DEALING WITH GRIEF

Understanding and Healing After the Loss of Someone You Love

JAMES WALKER

© Copyright 2019 - All rights reserved.

It is not legal to reproduce, duplicate, or transmit any part of this document in either electronic means or in printed format. Recording of this publication is strictly prohibited and any storage of this document is not allowed unless with written permission from the publisher except for the use of brief quotations in a book review.

CONTENTS

Fifteen Poems to Ease the Pain	v
Introduction	vii
Chapter One: Anatomy of Grief—The Five Stages	1
Chapter Two: You're Not Crazy—How Grief Manifests	11
Chapter Three: The Companionship Paradox—Accompanied, but Alone	18
Chapter Four: Double-Headed Snake: The Two Big Lies	28
Chapter Five: More Myths About Grief	36
Chapter Six: More Popular Grief Myths	61
Chapter Seven: Coping Mechanism: What Can I Do?	71
Chapter Eight: The Six Steps to Acceptance	101
Final Words	109
Author's Note	113
Fifteen Poems to Ease the Pain	115
References	117

FIFTEEN POEMS TO EASE THE PAIN

Thank you for purchasing this book.

There is nothing we can say to take away the pain you might be feeling now, but we hope these fifteen classic poems will help ease the grief at least a bit.

Go to the link below to download your gift.

https://mailchi.mp/e99e1518d1ad/fifteen-poems-to-ease-the-pain

INTRODUCTION

Are you mourning the loss of a loved one? Different people grieve in various ways, and there's no one right way to do it. It is important for you to go through the process and deal with the emptiness and anger you're feeling, though; otherwise, you might become consumed by the void that is opening within you.

Right now, it might seem like you'll never stop hurting, but once you come to terms with the death of your loved one, the pain will be manageable. Although no one mourns in the same way, there is a method you can use to accept what's happened and work through the process. What I've provided in this book are general steps that you can take, customizing them to fit your particular needs and the situation you are finding yourself in. But I want you to know something—I didn't write this book just to help you heal. I wrote it as a reminder that, even through loss and pain, there is always hope.

We humans tend to go through five stages of grief, though not necessarily in any given order. Some people may experience more than one stage simultaneously, whereas others may go from one stage to another, then back again. By learning to recognize what stage you're in, you'll be better equipped to work through it.

There's a lot of mental and emotional processing in this book, which means it won't be easy. That said, it's critical that you are kind to yourself. There's no right or wrong here, nor any proper emotion you should or shouldn't be feeling, and definitely no time limit. There's no stage where you're "supposed" to be at any given time. Grief is like any physical wound: it heals at its own pace, and all you can do is try and help it along.

Grief is a wound of the heart and the soul. It may be invisible, but it has an impact, not only internal, but also external. People who haven't suffered a significant loss before might not be aware that sorrow manifests itself both physically and mentally. In this book, we'll go over what those symptoms are, so you will be prepared when they show up. It's good to know what to expect because it'll help you know that what you're going through is perfectly normal.

As an example, if you've experienced loss recently, you might be conflicted by the paradox of both wanting to be left alone because you're grieving, yet craving for company. It's a situation you may not have experienced in the past that often leads to you believing you're doing it wrong or that something is wrong with you. It's another symptom of grief that is perfectly natural and normal but may seem like a problem, unless you're equipped to deal with it.

Because mourning is such a powerful process, there's a lot of information and advice out there. One of my missions with this book is to help you separate truth from fiction. Hopefully, I can arm you with the tools you need to avoid going in an unconstructive direction. There are a lot of myths to learn about when you're trying to understand your loss, along with a lot of outright lies.

One of the worst lies you'll probably hear is the one about letting go; that to heal and move forward... you need to let go of all the pain and memories. However, detachment is not the best way to cope and often results in more pain down the road. Allow yourself to hold your memories. Yes, there will be heartache associated with them, but the idea is for you to grow with it.

There are other myths about grieving that you may have run across that won't serve you in your journey either. By understanding what's happening in your mind and why people sometimes say the things they do when confronted with loss, you can then separate what will help you from what will hurt you.

Another important part of the process is simply learning how to cope with the loss of someone significant in your life. There are unhealthy coping mechanisms, such as turning to drugs and alcohol, but I will provide healthy ones that you can implement instead. Some may work for you and others may not, but you'll find methods you can use to help you deal with the pain productively rather self-destructively.

Finally, I'll discuss the six-step system to acceptance. This is a simple albeit powerful technique that you can use in your journey.

Again, everyone grieves differently. I'm not here to deliver some sort of universal truth. I can only speak from the heart and my experience to help you. I'm not a doctor. I have no MD or PhD, and I'm not a therapist. What I am is a man who has been in your shoes and knows the struggle.

Some years ago, I went through a significant loss in my life. As it does for so many of us, the sorrow put me in a very bad place for a long time, one where I couldn't function. I finally had to make the decision to stop fighting the pain. There's a reason the first part of the Serenity Statement is to accept the things you cannot change. I made the conscious choice to *understand* the pain instead and use it to grow as a person and move forward.

If you don't deal with your emotions, not only will grief impair your functioning in the short term, but it will do so in the long term as well. The emotions don't go away, no matter how much you try to hide them, push them down, or pretend they're not there. Only by accepting them and learning to cope can you learn to live life healthily. You can then create space within yourself for the loss, so you won't forget it, yet you'll be able to pick up the pieces, rebuild, and move forward.

How do I know this works? After coming face to face with loss myself, I ended up in a bad place, and denial and anger led me to start drinking heavily. As a consequence, I lost my job and pushed everyone away. I was unable to accept the cards I'd been dealt. My inability to face my new reality lasted a long time, and it took hitting rock bottom for me to finally get my act together.

I want to help others do the same. There's no reason for anyone else to go through what I went through, and I'm hoping to prevent other people like you from going down that same terrible road. Instead, you can learn about grief, emotions, and coping in a way that will lead you down the right path.

I'm not promising that your pain will go away because I know it won't. You probably know it won't either, and you probably also know the love that you shared with that significant person will also not go away. You'll carry them both with you. What I will promise is that there is hope of a normal life again, and you don't have to be destroyed by your sorrow. This book will show you how to understand what's happening and cope with both your loss and feelings about it.

The longer you put off dealing with your emotions, the harder it will be for you to figure out how to do so healthily, and the longer the loss will eat away at you. If you don't accept your pain and use it to grow, it could overtake your life and take you down that dark road. Don't let pain be the driver of your life; transform it into a companion instead.

Please join me on this journey as I take you down a long road, full of obstacles and sadness but also hope.

CHAPTER ONE: ANATOMY OF GRIEF—THE FIVE STAGES

Although everyone grieves a bit differently, there are typically five stages of the process. They were first named by Elizabeth Kubler-Ross in her seminal book, *On Death and Dying*. Don't feel bad if you don't experience them in this specific order, or if you have more than one at the same time. Although the stages are pretty universal, the order isn't necessarily. You'll also find that you may spend much more time in one compared to another, and that's also completely normal.

Although it's important to recognize the stages, it's also key for you to let go of the idea that there is one "right" way to mourn. Each person processes in a different way, so you may find yourself in a different stage three months after your loss than a friend or relative who's gone through a similar bereavement. Neither of you is wrong.

Not only that, but not everyone experiences every stage of grief. You might "skip" a phase, and that's also perfectly normal. When you think about these five stages, it's critical to remember that they're a general guideline and not step-by-step instructions. You might have one emotion one day and a completely different one the next, in a different order from what I've listed. The process isn't set in stone, and the way it happens for you is the right way for you.

However, the important thing for you during your bereavement is to recognize which stage you're in, as doing so will help you cope healthily. Because you're entering unknown territory, the power of your emotions might be unexpected or even frightening. Recognizing that you're experiencing perfectly normal episodes on your journey will make it easier on you. Understanding what you're experiencing at any given time can help you see what you need.

Another critical thing to remember is that no matter what you're feeling currently, as long as there's life, there's hope and vice versa. The death of someone close to us, especially when sudden, often causes people to think more carefully about their own life and mortality. You can make your own choices and take control of your life once you've journeyed through the process and understand and accept your emotions.

These five stages help us cope with the loss. It's the way that human brains process the difficult event of death. There are subconscious reasons for each phase that help keep us alive and moving, even through the sorrow. Every human brain is different, and that's why everyone has a different grieving process while following the outlines of the five-stage framework.

DENIAL

In this phase, you might feel numb and overwhelmed. It's pretty typical to say, "This can't be happening." Sometimes, the bereaved may even go so far as to deny that the death actually happened, coming up with various theories as to how the body might have been switched or the person is being hidden as part of a conspiracy or to protect them.

Denying that the death occurred is a way to protect us against the shock of the loss, so we only let in as much as we can handle at one time. Otherwise, we might not survive ourselves.

Other common responses are to ask, "How can I go on, if I even can?" or "Why should I go on when my loved one is no longer in my life?" Once you've started to ask questions like this, you're letting reality in, thus assisting in the healing process. Your denial starts to fade as you accept the death and begin to focus on how you will cope with it.

If you're not sure whether you're in denial, you can look at your behavior patterns and see if they match up with this phase. Often, you'll find yourself procrastinating or doing things mindlessly. You're distracted easily and seem to forget things a lot. You could be telling yourself that you're fine and keeping busy to avoid your feelings.

You may feel like you're going numb or shutting down. Sometimes, you might just feel confused or in shock. All of these are normal when you're going through denial.

ANGER

This one might be a scary emotion for you, particularly if you've gone great lengths to try to avoid it in the past. However, if you are feeling it, you need to acknowledge it and accept that you're angry at the loss. It is perfectly natural to feel that way, even if you don't consider yourself an angry person naturally.

Although society seems to focus on suppressing anger, here is a situation where you want to fully feel it, rather than trying to pretend it doesn't exist. As mentioned earlier, not everyone goes through each of these five stages, and you might be a person who doesn't move through the anger phase. But don't fool yourself into thinking you're missing it when in fact you're suppressing it, or trying to avoid dealing with it.

To heal, you need to accept each stage that you do go through fully. Trying to ignore emotions that are broiling beneath the surface will always blow up in your face in some fashion. Your anger may feel explosive and uncontrollable, which may make you nervous to admit to. However, the feelings don't go away just because you want them to. They go away when you acknowledge that you're feeling them and allow yourself to experience them. Whether you're concerned about your feelings of anger, your grieving process is the right time to let them out and recognize them for what they are.

You may feel abandoned by the person who died or angry with your friends, family, doctor who treated your loved one, god of your faith if you have one, and even yourself. In other words, there are a lot of targets for your anger, so don't be surprised if you want to lash out at someone who isn't connected to your loved one.

Your rage helps you feel anchored and may provide you with some strength while you otherwise have a sense of weakness during this time. It provides a structure that bridges the gap between your feeling of being lost and abandoned and your connection to the person you're grieving. It's often—though not always—the case that the intensity of your anger is proportional to your love for that person, even if you're directing it elsewhere.

Although a lot of arguing or getting into fights is normal in this phase, you may also be more cynical or pessimistic than usual. You may notice you've become more sarcastic or irritable, are drinking or using more drugs, or are more aggressive or passive-aggressive.

In addition to identifying your rage, you may also feel like you're out of control. You may sense more frustration or resentment, and you can find yourself more impatient as well.

These are strong indicators that you're in the anger stage of the process.

BARGAINING

This stage is full of the "What ifs" and "If onlys." For example, "What if I spend the rest of my life feeding the homeless? Then I can wake up from this terrible dream and my loved one will be back here with me." Sometimes—particularly if the person was ill for a long time—you may have tried to make a similar trade to keep them alive and healthy.

After a significant death, it's common to want to go back in time and stop the death from happening. If only the lump had been found earlier, the person had controlled their blood pressure, or the car stopped before it went through the red light. The "if onlys" are usually accompanied by guilt—that you didn't insist on a doctor's visit or had been in the car and told them to stop. You're trying to think what you could have done differently to prevent it and where you might be at fault.

All this is an attempt to avoid the pain of the loss. It helps us feel like we're in control and that there was a reason the death happened. In this stage, the brain is focused on the past.

Key signals that you're in this stage involve your thinking. For example, you may be ruminating about the past or future, and in the latter, predicting chaos. You might be worrying and overthinking. Comparing yourself to others and judging people harshly, including yourself, often occur at this time.

Emotions during the bargaining stage are often things like guilt and shame. You may feel insecure, frightened, or anxious. During this phase, it's common to blame yourself and others. Although these feelings may seem threatening or scary, they're normal. Allow yourself to experience them fully as a way of healing.

DEPRESSION

Quite often, you'll find that you move from the past into the present, where the reality sets in and the pain you were trying to avoid rears its head. It may feel like this stage will last forever, and you'll never be able to get out of it.

Bear in mind that this is a completely reasonable reaction to a significant loss. It's not something to be fixed. Further on, we'll discuss the difference between grief and clinical depression, but this phase of the process is natural and appropriate. Someone near and dear to you is gone and not coming back, so of course you're feeling despair and sadness.

In this phase, the truth of the matter really settles in. You might feel lost and withdraw from others. You might not be sure whether you can or should go on from there. You may be wondering—what's the point of living without my loved one?

This is another emotion that people often try to avoid, ignore, or suppress, particularly when you don't see how you'll ever feel better or enjoy life again. Just as with anger, however, you need to recognize fully that you're feeling this way and allow yourself to experience it while it's happening. It won't last forever, but if you're feeling it, you must accept it to heal.

Here, again, people may find themselves tempted to drown out their pain or take the easy way out. Other indicators for the depression phase include crying and a lack of energy or motivation. You may discover that your sleeping and eating habits change.

It's typical to feel overwhelmed and helpless during this time. You might also feel hopeless, sad, disappointed, and despairing. Although you may be worried that these feelings will last for the rest of your life, they won't. This is a step on the way to healing, even though it may seem as if it will never end, or is too sad to bear for long.

ACCEPTANCE

People who haven't gone through the grief process might think that this is the stage where you can get over it or that you're now perfectly fine with the death. However, no one who has ever lost a loved one is ever perfectly okay with it or completely over their bereavement. The significant person will always be in your heart and mind.

Instead, at this stage, you recognize the situation for what it is. Your loved one is not coming back, and you know you must go forward in your life without that person in it. Your life has changed permanently, and now you need to learn how to adjust to your new normal. You'll never replace that person, but you will go on to make new connections and rebuild your life.

Once you understand that your life will forever be different, you can use your experience to help you grow as a person and evolve into your best self. Accepting that your loved one is gone doesn't mean that you will ever forget them. Moving forward with your life is not betraying them, either. You'll always have your memories with you, and you can take them out any time you like. Staying mired in your grief means that you stop growing as a person, which your loved one would not have wanted you to do.

The Serenity Statement is simply, "Grant me the serenity to accept the things I cannot change, the courage to change the things I can, and the wisdom to know the difference" (Sherman, 2017).[1] When you ultimately accept the new reality of life, you may feel more at peace with the world, even as you feel the pain of your sorrow. However, you can't achieve serenity without the first piece of acceptance.

Here you'll come back to the present and be able to stay there. You can tolerate the feelings you're having and can be vulnerable with trusted people. You begin again to engage with the world as it is instead of wishing there were some other way. You'll communicate honestly and be more mindful in your speech and actions.

Finally, you can feel some self-compassion and even pride in who you are, now that you've come through the process. Although you will still have sad days and times when you mourn your loved one, you'll accept your feelings and be mindful of them.

DEPRESSION VS. GRIEF

Depression is common to those who are going through the grieving process. However, it's different from clinical depression during this time. Sometimes, people have difficulties telling the difference between the two. Seeking counsel can help with both experiences, but anyone who's clinically depressed may need additional help. There are certain symptoms for each that can help you decide if you're not sure which one you're experiencing.

When you're grieving, you'll find yourself on a daily, possibly even hourly rollercoaster of emotions. You'll have many different emotions from one moment to the next, and you'll have both bad and good days throughout the journey. You'll even feel happiness every once in a while and enjoy some pleasant times.

By contrast, clinical depression usually manifests in feeling despair or emptiness consistently. You may feel intense guilt or worthlessness, and you may not be functioning the way you should at school, work, or home. It's also possible that you'll be hearing or seeing things that aren't there.

Either way, there is help for you. Later in the book, I'll discuss some ways you can cope with your loss when grieving. If you think you recognize the clinical depression symptoms, you'll want to talk to a professional to get help. You can always talk to a professional if you're grieving as well, especially if you end up so intensely preoccupied with the death that you can't resume other activities.

COMPLICATED GRIEF

Most people can go through the bereavement journey healthily in about a year (Mayo Clinic, 2017).[2] However, some may stay stuck and be unable to move on from one or more stages for longer than a year, which is known as complicated grief. The emotions in this situation can be so painful and severe that you're unable to recover and live your life again. You cannot heal because you're in a heightened state of ongoing mourning.

You might find yourself trying constantly to rewrite the loss into something different or deny that you're grieving. Ruminating about the past is actually a way of avoiding painful truths, both in grief and life.

If, after a year, you cannot reach acceptance of the death of your loved one, you may need to ask for help from a professional.

CHAPTER SUMMARY

The five stages of grief may not be experienced by everyone going through the bereavement journey, and you may not go through them in the order listed above.

- The five stages are denial, anger, bargaining, depression, and acceptance, though it's not a linear process and you might jump back and forth between them.
- Although the feelings might seem frightening or something you'd rather not deal with, they're perfectly normal.
- To heal, it's critical that you allow yourself to experience your feelings rather than trying to suppress or ignore them.
- Clinical depression is different from the grieving process, and if you are exhibiting symptoms, it's wise to go to a professional for help.
- Complicated grief occurs when you cannot rebuild your life after a year or so of mourning.

In the next chapter, you will learn about how grief can manifest, whether obvious or not.

CHAPTER TWO: YOU'RE NOT CRAZY—HOW GRIEF MANIFESTS

In popular culture, grief is often represented by crying, which is a perfectly normal reaction! However, there are many more ways in which grief can manifest itself in the body in addition to crying. Not all of them are mental or emotional, either. Some ways in which you might feel it are physical.

Because these manifestations aren't often described or mentioned in popular culture, when people start experiencing them, they might worry that they're going crazy or they're abnormal. However, these manifestations are very normal, and you don't need to worry that you're going off the deep end if you start seeing some of them appear. They're an indicator that you're going through the process just as you should. You're in the same boat as I was and many others who need to heal after the death of a loved one.

Just like with the five stages, you may not experience all of these manifestations. However, it's critical to know what they are, so if you do sense them, you know they're a consequence of the death of your loved one. You don't need to worry or be concerned that you're the only one going through them. Although people around you may not be experiencing the same manifestations that you are, other people certainly do when they're faced with that kind of loss.

Why does grief manifest in these different ways? It interrupts the normal function of the brain. Since mind and body are tightly linked, changes to the brain usually result in changes to the body as well. Bereavement causes changes in how the brain releases mood-regulating neurochemicals like serotonin and dopamine, along with other networks and nerves in the brain. Hormones are also altered as a result of the process.

The prefrontal cortex is the region of the human brain where reason, logic, and decision-making occur. It's the "thinking" part of the brain and is affected by grief as well. Memory, concentration, and other functions that rely on the prefrontal cortex can be changed by grief.

All the body's systems are affected by grief. Many of the most common symptoms seem to originate in the cardiovascular, immune, nervous, and digestive systems. However, they can also manifest in others, such as the renal (kidney), musculoskeletal, and reproductive systems. Essentially, your entire body and brain may be affected by your bereavement.

Whatever manifestations of grief happen for you are temporary while you're going through the process, so don't be concerned that you may become unable to function normally for the rest of your life! The more you can recognize, acknowledge, and accept your feelings, the better you'll be able to heal. Once you can move on again, the manifestations of pain that you've been experiencing will dissipate.

PHYSICAL SIGNALS

Emotional pain is activated in the same regions of the brain as physical pain, which is part of the reason why you might have physical symptoms during your healing process (Hairston, 2019).[3] Grief increases inflammation in the body, which will make any underlying conditions worse as well. It depletes the immune system, so you'll be more likely to fall ill from infections. The stress of the pain can increase blood pressure and the presence of blood clots. It can even change the heart itself, leading to "broken-heart syndrome" with the same symptoms as a heart attack.

Additional physical symptoms of grief include:

- Dry mouth.
- Headaches or other aches and pains.
- Shortness of breath, in which case, you should call your doctor to make sure there's nothing more serious going on.
- Chest pains, which may mean you might want to call emergency services.
- Stomach pain.
- Nausea.
- Fatigue.
- Being overly sensitive to noise and/or light.
- Increased heart rate.
- Decreased appetite.
- Increased appetite, soothing emotions with food.
- Panic attacks.
- Muscle weakness.
- General heaviness in the body.

OTHER MANIFESTATIONS OF GRIEF

In the last chapter, you learned about some of the emotions and behaviors that you may exhibit during the various stages of the process, such as anger, distraction, forgetfulness, and helplessness. Yet, there are more ways that you might find grief in your life that can surprise or make you fearful.

Dreams or even nightmares about the deceased are common, particularly when you're still working through the process and a lot of your conscious time is spent thinking about them. It's natural that they're present in your subconscious mind as well.

Another sleep manifestation is insomnia. You may be finding it very hard to get to sleep or stay asleep. Conversely, you may instead sleep too much, whether due to the extreme fatigue that often sets in or sadness and depression you're feeling. Sleep can help you avoid the pain of consciousness, so you try not to be awake for as long as you can.

Anxiety is often present, not just in the one stage. Humans are social beings, and we form attachments to others. This attachment is necessary to survive, and once we've formed an attachment to someone else, the bond exists, even when the other person isn't there. When that person dies, you must learn to live with the bond that still exists. Anxiety and numbing are often the result.

You might also experience what are known as "grief pangs," which are short periods of intense yearning for the person who's gone and the distress of that painful emotion. You'll be preoccupied with thoughts of your loved one and a strong longing—even searching—for them. These pangs might result in a feeling of severe emptiness but help recover them in memory.

Another experience is feeling less safe in the world. The person who's gone may have been a significant source of safety for you. Or they may not have been. Either way, the loss of a loved one often causes people to feel unmoored from reality or that they've lost an anchor to the world.

You might feel relieved that the person is gone. Many people are worried when they're feeling this particular emotion, but again, it's perfectly natural. You're relieved that their pain and suffering is over, so it doesn't mean that you're a monster or didn't care about them.

Maybe you're feeling distanced from everything. It's most common right after death occurs, and you feel detached from your life. As with all feelings, it will eventually dissipate yet allow yourself to notice this feeling of indifference as you experience it.

Are you unable to concentrate on what you're doing? Many people find that their minds keep going back to the death or memories they have of their loved one and have a hard time focusing on what they're supposed to be doing in the present.

Related to the problem of concentration is your ability to drive. Steering a vehicle that weighs thousands of pounds safely requires focus and decision-making, both of which can be impaired by grief. Some people may find themselves crying uncontrollably behind the wheel, whereas others may notice a slower reaction time to what's happening on the road.

Likewise, you may have trouble with planning and organizing. These functions rely on the prefrontal cortex function, and as I mentioned earlier, grief can alter this region of the brain as well. As a result of your inability to plan and organize, you might be concerned about your ability to make decisions or become unsure of yourself.

You may discover signs of restlessness or nervousness as well. You tap or drum your fingers more often or pace back and forth. Your hands and feet may be clammy or sweaty, or you may experience numbness and tingling in them. You may fidget and have a hard time sitting still or be in one place for a long time.

One of the physical manifestations noted earlier is increased eating, which could lead to weight gain. You could also become heavier due to eating too much junk food and not enough nutritional food. You may also find yourself eating out more often and isolating from friends and family who would otherwise encourage healthier behavior.

By contrast, a decreased appetite can lead to weight loss. You may not have the energy to cook food or even pick up the phone or drive anywhere to pick up healthy food. You could be so caught up in the details of the funeral or managing the estate plan that you don't have time to sit down for good meals.

Sometimes when you're grieving, you may find that the temperature of wherever you happen to be is just not right. You're either too hot or too cold. You could experience chills, sweat more than usual, or sweat at night.

In addition to stomach pain and nausea, people often notice more digestive tract issues because grief can affect the gastrointestinal system too. Constipation or diarrhea are common, as is heartburn and acid reflux. You might feel like there is a hole or emptiness in your stomach. Some people develop Irritable Bowel Syndrome as a result of their bereavement.

Later in chapter seven, I'll show you what you can do to alleviate some of these manifestations and do your best to cope with what's going on. For now, accept that grief is affecting you mentally, emotionally, and physically, all of which are natural when on this journey.

CHAPTER SUMMARY

Grief may affect every system in your body and mind, and it manifests in ways that may come as a surprise. Recognizing your symptoms as normal will help you work toward your healing journey.

- Many people think about grief as being purely

emotional and mental, but it shows up in the body as well.
- Physical signs may appear in any area of the body, including the heart, stomach, muscles, and eyes.
- Grief often causes changes in your normal habits, such as sleeping and eating.
- There are many other ways in which sorrow may show up in your life, and all of them are perfectly natural for anyone who has experienced the death of a loved one.

In the next chapter, you will learn about the paradox of wanting people around, while at the same time wanting to be isolated.

CHAPTER THREE: THE COMPANIONSHIP PARADOX— ACCOMPANIED, BUT ALONE

When a significant person in your life is gone, you may feel like you're in uncharted territory—somewhere off the map where no one else has ever been before. The people around you may be unaware of how deeply the death has affected you and may not even understand what grief is actually like.

People who have never experienced the death of a loved one have no idea what it's like. If this is the first one you've had in your life, you may be shocked at what you're feeling, how strong your emotions are running, and how big the hole in your life actually is. No one else can imagine it unless they've been to this uncharted territory themselves or are currently wandering somewhere off the map.

That's why you may be surprised at the reactions of the people around you. They have no idea about the emptiness and might expect you to be back to normal after a few days off. They may expect you to be sad and despairing all the time, when in fact, your emotions are on a rollercoaster, where you're laughing one minute at a funny joke and then crying a minute later. Don't allow them to define the pace of your path to rebuilding, and don't let their inability to understand what you're going through make you feel bad about your emotions.

You may want to be around other people, who take your mind off the pain and distract you from the feelings you might be trying to avoid. On the other hand, their ignorance about what you're going through drives you away from them. You could be feeling drained and lethargic, and you're just not up to being around people. Possibly all of these emotions are occurring pretty much at the same time, so you're wondering, what gives?

PEOPLE ARE SOCIAL BEINGS

We humans evolved to live in small groups, and that's how we survived as a species. Unlike other predators, we don't have as much strength nor the sharp teeth or long claws. We also aren't particularly physically large compared to other animals who might have wanted to hunt and kill us. We were saved by our highly developed brains and endurance.

Compared to other predators, we can keep moving for a long time. A cheetah can sprint between 50 and 80 miles per hour, and a lion can also hit 50. However, neither of them can keep up that speed for an hour. A human may be unable to run that fast, but one can chase their prey for hours and exhaust them. Humans can also use their developed brains to project into the future and guess where their prey will be accurately—near a watering hole at a certain time of day, for example, if they lose sight during the hunt.

Like other social animals, humans can work together to get their food. People can also work together to build dwellings that protect them from the elements and other predators. Over time, humans working together figured out how to make fire to cook their meat, explored new lands, developed language to communicate, and fashioned ever more sophisticated tools.

Why am I talking about how we evolved? There are two aspects to it that are particularly relevant to those of us who have suffered a severe loss. One is the idea of physical endurance, and the other is the social aspect of humanity.

As you saw in the previous chapter, grief manifests itself physically in a variety of ways. Some people report that their bodies feel extremely heavy. Or you might be experiencing fatigue, lethargy, or a complete lack of energy. Even talking to someone on the phone or trying to fix a meal seems like an impossible amount of work right now.

No matter how badly your body feels, it's evolved to withstand a pretty hefty amount of punishment. You may be wondering if you can go on physically because you have so many aches and pains or other debilitating symptoms. Knowing that your body is built to keep going and has that endurance can help you during those days when you're not sure your body will let you heal.

The social aspect that we share as human beings is a key part of the paradox I mentioned. People want to be accompanied by others to some degree because of our very nature as *Homo sapiens*.

COMPANIONSHIP

As you might expect, given that we evolved in small groups, being at least somewhat social is baked right into our DNA. If you're an introvert, you might think it's not true. However, introverts need friends and connections too. They just need fewer people in their circle of trusted people than extroverts do. An introvert can be perfectly happy with just a handful of people in their innermost circle, but extroverts typically need many more than that. Either way, both kinds of people (as well as ambiverts, who are in the middle) still need some people around them they can trust.

You can see why you might have the need to be around others during this time. If nothing else, it's because humans crave social interaction. Your desire for companionship might be higher or lower or flip back and forth between the extremes. As a reminder, everyone's process is unique to them, so whatever you're experiencing will be normal for you.

Much of the difference between introverts and extroverts comes down to dopamine, one of the pleasure neurochemicals. It turns out that introverts tend to be more sensitive to it, which means they need less of it to feel the effects (Granneman, 2020).[4] Too much social activity, like a loud party with lots of people and bright lights, is overstimulating to introverts and wears them out faster. By contrast, extroverts need more dopamine to feel happy, so a stimulating party is right up their alley because the dopamine release for them is just right.

In the previous chapter, you also learned that neurochemicals like dopamine are affected by grief. If you're an extrovert, you could end up feeling overstimulated by people, which normally doesn't happen when you're not grieving, so you want more time to yourself. As an introvert, you might be surprised at your desire to spend more time with others than you usually would because you want more companionship.

In some cases, your natural tendencies could be heightened by your sorrow, there's no effect on your need to be accompanied by others. All these things are perfectly normal, given the process you're going through.

LONELINESS

In some Western cultures, grief isn't much talked about, and certainly very few people discuss how to move through the process. In addition, extroversion is celebrated and encouraged. There's high reward in being social and expending a lot of energy in meeting new people and making new friends and connections. So, you may be feeling pressure from those around you to get back to work and be your normal, cheery, outgoing self.

Instead, here you are with this new, enormous hole or emptiness. No one around you seems to understand what you're dealing with. Not only that, but a person you loved and bonded with is gone. You're realizing just how much you've lost now that they're no longer with you. The world is an emptier place without them.

In other words, you have two distinct reasons for being lonely. One is that your loved one is gone, makes you lonely, in and of itself. In addition, you probably feel that you've lost a portion (if not all) of your support system too. People don't know how to deal with your loss, thus they want you to hurry up and recover so they don't have to feel your pain.

They may not know how to deal with it, and as a result, drop you completely. That's their inability to grapple with the situation, but it often leaves you feeling like you're the one who did something wrong; it is because they believe you didn't manage your grief in a way they find acceptable.

That also leads to intense feelings of loneliness. You think it's just you in this uncharted territory, and it's you alone without a guide or map. You're not wrong for feeling this way, by the way. When you don't have the social support that's so important for survival, it's natural to feel this kind of loneliness. Fortunately, you have a map in the form of this book, but take all the time you need to acknowledge and accept your loneliness. There is no timetable, so move at a pace that's right for you.

ISOLATION

Another consequence of feeling pressured by others or even yourself is to turn away from people. They're letting you down, so why would you want to be around them? Instead, you reflect on your loss and get in touch with the emotions you're feeling. It's not necessarily a bad thing, but it can lead into a downward spiral. You need to draw away from others to heal, but then you feel lonely, which makes you feel isolated, and so on.

Another reason people who are bereaved might isolate is due to the extreme fatigue that often accompanies the grief itself. When you're low on energy, it's difficult to pick up the phone to call someone, get on the video conference, or even knock on your friendly nearby neighbor's door to have a chat. In this case, it's probably not intentional, but still results in being alone by yourself.

Now that you're in uncharted territory, you might simply not feel as comfortable hanging out with others from your life before you experienced the death of your loved one. This can be particularly true when the loss has left you questioning who you really are as a person, which is also common with grief. Do you want to hang out with the same people, whose ideas and conversations no longer seem quite as important as they did before? When you're feeling uncomfortable with former situations and friends, it's much easier to isolate yourself.

And, especially for those who are introverts, being isolated can be the usual tendency or inclination when you're not feeling well, either mentally or physically. It seems natural to hide away from the world when you're processing intense emotions.

Just as people may feel lonely and want to surround themselves with others, some may prefer to isolate and stay away from everyone else. Isolation might also be the consequence of other issues that arise during the grieving process. You might find yourself ping ponging back and forth between wanting to be by yourself and not wanting to be alone, or you may find you've settled on one as opposed to the other.

Whichever you're feeling is a part of your personal journey, and none of them are "wrong." Remember that your journey is specific to you personally, so don't be concerned about what's happening.

> *"To be, or not to be, that is the question."*
>
> — HAMLET, WILLIAM SHAKESPEARE

When you add in the word "alone," you have the essence of the paradox. To be alone, or not to be alone, and sometimes both at once. As you've probably discovered during this process, people who haven't been through this type of loss really don't get it. They question you or get offended when you express your need to get away from other people for a while.

While you're grieving, your healing process comes first. Don't worry too much about how others are feeling about the transition you find yourself going through. Respect your feelings and acknowledge them; recognizing that there's nothing wrong with you will always be a better start than what everyone else tells you.

When struggling with this paradox, there will be a few things that can help you work through it and get the support you need. After too much time in isolation, it can get hard to get back out into the "real" world. Therefore, it's critical that you reach out for support and let people know how they can do that for you because most of them won't know what you need. Also, let them know that when you need to process by yourself and that it's not personal; it's just a part of your process.

Later in the book, you'll find the chapter on healthy coping mechanisms, but here are some ways you can communicate with others about your need or lack thereof for companionship. You'll need to identify a few trusted people that you can rely on.

Note that these people won't necessarily be the same people you felt you could count on before your loss. If your best friend hasn't called in to see how you're doing, they're probably not reliable for reasons of their own. Be as objective as you can about people in your circle who will lift you up and not drag you down due to their own loneliness or bitterness.

They'll need to be there when you want or need to talk. Sometimes, reaching out to someone who is also grieving your loved one can be helpful because you can share pleasant memories, and they may need to talk too. The people you trust can also be your buffer when you can't handle all the well-wishers, and let others know when you need to be alone for a while.

It's likely that such a person will have experienced a similar situation in their lives, so they understand this paradox very well and won't judge or criticize you for it. If you do have people in your life who are criticizing the way you're grieving, cease contact if you can. Sometimes, unfortunately, they might be your supervisor or colleagues that you can't drop for some time. However, if it's possible, try and stay in touch only with those who support you.

If you enjoy having people around you and need outside contact to heal and help alleviate the loneliness, that's also perfectly OK. Just ensure that they won't be critical or judgemental or pretend that nothing's wrong. Having friends and acquaintances like that, no matter how well-meaning they are, won't help you heal. No matter how lonely you're feeling, you don't need to be with just anyone who has a pulse. Choose wisely and seek out the people who will lift you up.

Whether or not you want to be alone, consider a support group. There are many available for those who are grieving. You might even find one that's specific to your loss, such as parents whose children are gone. You can search for them online. It's a good idea for many people in your situation.

Groups like these are especially helpful when you want to be around people, but not necessarily the ones in your life who don't seem to get it. You could be wanting to isolate but are concerned that you might be spending too much time by yourself, or you don't have the energy to talk. In many group settings, you can just listen until you're ready. Some cultures, including pop culture, may make fun of support groups or claim that they're useless. You won't know unless you go, and they have many benefits that will help you heal (Mayo Clinic, 2020).[5] On the other hand, if you really don't want to attend a group meeting, you don't have to.

Although the paradox between wanting to be alone during your grieving process while wanting to be in contact with other humans may seem irrational, it's normal after the death of a loved one. Give yourself permission to feel either or both of these desires and look for support from trusted people and those who understand your situation due to their own experiences.

CHAPTER SUMMARY

Whether you're an introvert or extrovert, during the grieving process, you may want to be alone for a time, be with other people, or both. It's all part of your journey and is normal in bereavement.

- Humans evolved in small groups, and being connected to others is how we survived, which is why we need companionship now.
- Many of us going through the experience feel that we're alone in the world because it seems others have abandoned us or they just don't understand.
- You may isolate because you need to process emotions, you're too tired to reach out, you're uncomfortable with your circumstances, or other reasons.
- You may want to be left alone, with others, or both, and there are ways you can respect these emotions at any given time, often with the help of others.

In the next chapter, you will learn about the two big lies you might often hear during your journey.

CHAPTER FOUR: DOUBLE-HEADED SNAKE: THE TWO BIG LIES

You've no doubt noticed by now that the word "death" is almost considered dirty in our culture. Although it is the inevitable end for all of us, many don't acknowledge it. People tend to avoid the subject as often as they can because it makes them uncomfortable.

In previous decades, the relatives of the decedent sometimes lied or omitted the cause of death, as if it were somehow shameful to be stricken with cancer or other diseases. This continued, even into the 1980s with the AIDS epidemic. It is less common today, although the focus is on the disease or condition itself and survivors are celebrated. Even with these cultural advances, however, death is still something to be tucked behind the curtain and not spoken of, except maybe at the funeral. At the very least, the topic is avoided.

In other words, it's hard to have conversations about death. Even well-meaning friends and colleagues don't know what to say or how to offer comfort. They don't know how to talk with the surviving friends and relatives about the loss of the loved one. They may want to support you, but they fall back on platitudes because that's all they've ever heard.

So, there are two big lies when it comes to the grieving process. One is external—that people will tell you in the mistaken belief that it will help you to heal; and the other is internal: when you tell yourself to take control of an uncontrollable situation and heal from it. Without a map to guide you through your grief, you're left to figure out how to heal on your own.

Lie #1: Letting go is the secret to healing from your loss.

Another consequence of being unable to have conversations about death and dying is that people are uncomfortable in its presence. Someone who knew your loved one but wasn't as close as you are might be sad about it. However, they can compartmentalize the death much easier and not think or feel too deeply about it. Most people don't want to think about their own mortality and shy away from it.

On the other hand, you're a visible representative of your loved one to others. That often brings their own mortality uncomfortably close, and they don't want to deal with it. So, they would prefer that you hurry up and deal with it yourself, so they don't have to be reminded of it. They may even drop you entirely from their contacts.

So, they tell you just to let go of it. Let go of the person, death, and your grief. To them, it seems like the easiest way for you to "get over it" and come back to the self that you were before your loved one died.

Sure, detachment is great in theory, but it's not possible, and what you should let go of is any pressure to deal with your bereavement in a prescribed way, particularly from anyone who has no idea what you're going through.

As you learned in an earlier chapter, you'll still feel the bonds to someone you were connected to, even when that person is no longer with you. Letting go of that connection isn't a realistic expectation because the human mind doesn't work that way.

Many people in your situation will want to believe this lie. Let's face it, grief is painful emotionally, mentally, and physically. You want to get rid of this pain because sometimes, you're afraid it will take over and you'll feel nothing but intense grief and sorrow until the end of your days. If someone is telling you that letting go will bring you relief, it's natural to reach for that remedy.

However, the grief will never leave you, and neither will the loss of your loved one. You will always carry them with you. Simply letting go of them isn't an option. What does happen—and I can attest to this personally—is that over time, your grief will lessen. You will eventually be able to talk about them and think of them without the intense sorrow you currently feel.

You won't feel the emptiness they've left every day. Though sometimes, you will feel that absence within you, it won't be as debilitating as it is now. Your grief becomes a part of you—not an overwhelming force that disrupts your life. Although it may seem improbable now, that's where your healing journey will take you.

Set aside this notion of detachment and letting go. It doesn't serve you. You may understand why people say it, but you don't need to believe it. The truth may be more painful in the short term, but it will liberate you. Recognize that the bond is there—even though the person you love is no longer with you—and ignore those who tell you to let go.

Lie #2: I could have prevented this tragedy.

Here is where you might get sucked into a spiral of mind games. This lie is typically one that we tell ourselves, not something that comes from the outside world. It is also common in bereaved people because it satisfies the need that the human brain has for *cognitive closure*. Our brains want answers—it doesn't like ambiguity or uncertainty. Even as children, human beings will not only create an explanation for the unexpected but hold onto them as if they were known facts (Konnikova, 2013).[6] We live in an uncertain world, and this is one of the ways we've evolved to cope with it.

One way of manifesting control over a situation is to avoid it. You may have seen this yourself if you've ever heard someone announce they were suffering from a serious disease or condition. For example, upon hearing that someone has lung cancer, the first question people tend to ask is if they smoked. If they have diabetes, what did they eat? How did the person break their bones, need surgery, etc.? You might even have asked the question yourself upon hearing news like this. Not intending to make the other person feel bad or guilty, but to find out what you need to do or not to prevent their diagnosis. We victim blame naturally. You may ask yourself or the other person, "What should I be doing differently to avoid that same situation?"

The question is similar to the one people often ask themselves when grieving the death of a loved one. But, instead of focusing on what you can do now to avoid a future issue, you're asking what you could have done back then to prevent your loved one from dying.

You know rationally that you can't turn back time. There's no time machine you can use to rewind and change what happened, but your brain wants that cognitive closure of being able to find the cause of death, which results in trying to figure out how it could have been avoided.

Everyone has a baseline of their general need for this closure. For some people, it's higher, whereas for others, it's lower. It depends on several factors, such as your difficulty with ambiguity (those who can tolerate more certainty aren't driven as much to seek closure), need for predictability and order, and so on. Whatever your natural level happens to be, external circumstances can increase this need, such as more stress or a crisis (Konnikova, 2013).[7] You can see why you might be more driven to find explanations—no matter how illogical—when under the stress of grief.

Although it's perfectly natural, it still won't serve you because the human brain tends to latch onto whatever explanation it has invented, and you can get stuck on the idea that you could have done something differently. That means you can't move forward because you've become attached to the idea that the death could have been avoided. You cannot reach acceptance—which is where you need to be to rebuild your life—when you're still stuck in the past.

The brain can derive these explanations spontaneously, so you might not even be thinking about it consciously when the "solution" to the death comes to your attention. That means you might not even understand that you're telling yourself this lie; it doesn't seem like anything that you created on purpose.

If that's the case, how can you tell? Fortunately, the signs are pretty obvious—you'll recognize the phrases "what if" and "if only" recurring often in your thoughts. If you find you're having difficulty with this, there are a few things you can do that will help you stop the cycle.

1. *Write them down on paper*

Journaling is a way to manage stress and anxiety as well. You do need to write them by hand because handwriting activates the brain in a way that typing won't (Lumauig, 2015).[8] If it makes you feel better, you could even purchase a nice journal that you would write in, but a plain pencil and paper is just fine too.

Write until you're done. When you feel that there's nothing left in your brain, and you have no more thoughts about your loved one's death, you'll be done for that journal entry. The first few times you write, you may discover that it takes you a long time to finish because you have so much to write about. That's okay. Many people find they cycle through a lot of emotions, and that's fine too. Just write until you're through it.

2. Talk to someone (not necessarily a therapist)

The "what ifs" and "if onlys" are inward thoughts that tend to lead to rumination, which means dwelling on the past. Taking productive action is a way to help you stop these mind games. In this case, a good action is to turn outward and connect with someone else. This gives you something else to think about.

It's also fine if you want to reach out to someone else who also knew your loved one to reminisce. Although you may be talking about the past, you're not ruminating or getting stuck on "what ifs" but about things that actually happened. It can help you work toward acceptance.

3. Help someone else

This is another excellent way to take productive action. Focus on someone else's problems or issues and help them solve it. It's a great way to get out of your head while someone else receives the help they need.

Hardwired into the human brain is pleasure in helping

others, which is probably a consequence of how we evolved in social groups. It reduces the stress-related activity in your brain, which will be helpful when grieving (Bergland, 2016).[9]

By stopping these negative thoughts and taking other actions, you can keep moving forward into your new future. Getting stuck in rumination about the past or figuring out how you could have prevented it, you also get stuck on your path to healing.

The longer you continue with unhealthy coping mechanisms (including believing these two big lies and other myths you'll learn about later), the longer your journey will be. Make the process easier on yourself and focus on the things that will help you: acknowledging and accepting your emotions as they come, discovering healthy ways to cope, and finding support from trustworthy and reliable people.

CHAPTER SUMMARY

There are two lies—one external and one internal—that will prevent you from moving forward on your journey.

- One lie often comes from outside sources, which tells you that you just need to let go of everything to heal.
- The second is one you tell yourself, which is that you could have done something differently that would have avoided the loss.
- There are a number of ways to get yourself out of the vicious cycle of "what ifs" and "if onlys," such as journaling, talking to a friend, and helping someone else.
- Although both these lies are understandable and normal, neither of them will help you on your path to healing.

In the next chapter, you will learn about more grief myths that won't serve you.

CHAPTER FIVE: MORE MYTHS ABOUT GRIEF

In the previous chapter, you learned about how our current culture supports lies and misconceptions about the bereavement process. You might be searching the Internet, looking for resources in your library, or watching entertainment that deals with the subject. It's important that you have some grounding in what can help you and what might hurt you as you travel along your path.

If you have already done some of this research and believed one of the myths that you find in this or the next chapter, don't feel bad. This may all be new to you, and some of these myths may feel good. They say in the gym, "No pain, no gain," and that's sometimes true on your grief journey as well.

By accepting and acknowledging the pain of losing your loved one fully, you'll find it dissipating faster. On the other hand, when you try to ignore or squish it down to where you can't feel it, you actually slow down your journey because that's not how emotional pain works.

Everyone wants to feel better, and our society tends to support quick fixes as well. People who care about you want you to heal, and they don't want to see you suffer or your pain because it hurts them too. You can see how they might want you to do something that seems like a quick fix but doesn't actually help. Make sure your journey is actually healing for you and not just putting forth the mere *appearance* of healing.

Many of these myths—if you end up believing them—will make you feel like you're "doing it wrong," which can be very harmful to you. Already, you have a huge emptiness in your life that you're trying to deal with, and adding to it feelings of guilt will make you feel that much worse. I say this because you might run across a myth that we won't explore here in this book, and it's crucial that you don't place obstacles in your way. Hopefully, these words will provide you with the tools to tell the useful and harmful apart.

If you do run across something that makes you feel worse about how you're handling your bereavement, recognize it as a perfect example of something that's not helping you and might need to reconsider in terms of effectiveness and truthfulness. If someone says something to you that makes you feel guilty, wrong, or ashamed, then ignore them. They don't know what they're talking about. They've probably never experienced what you're going through, so why should you listen to them? They may have good intentions, but that's irrelevant. Focus on that which you can do to move yourself forward instead.

Myth: Each of the five stages of grief are experienced linearly.

You learned a little about this in the first chapter that discussed these stages, but it's worth mentioning again because this idea is so pervasive. Most psychology journals have dispensed with this myth, but you might hear it from other people or see it referenced in pop culture. You're not wrong if you don't go through each of the five stages, experience them in a different order, or are in one stage and you go back to a previous one. They are all normal and part of your specific path.

Elizabeth Kubler-Ross developed them based on research she did with people who were dying and not with people struggling with bereavement (Mendoza, 2018).[10] Psychologists and therapists now realize that it doesn't work the same way for people who are grieving and can fluctuate between the stages by the hour, sometimes even by the minute.

Myth: Grief is like a cold—you get a little better each day until it goes away.

Just as grief doesn't follow a linear progression through the five stages, it also doesn't continue to improve daily and step by step. You'll have days when you're feeling fine, maybe even enjoying some time with friends or doing an activity you love. Then, the next day you may be feeling numb, angry, or sad.

Putting any kind of timeframe or boundary on your healing process is counterproductive. You'll feel like you're one step closer to acceptance, then believe you've taken two steps back. It will take the time that it takes. Although you can help move it forward with healthy coping mechanisms (which we'll discuss later), you can't direct how long it will take or the progression that you'll make.

The grief doesn't go away. It won't be such an active part of your life later, and you can then get on with your life without being stopped in your tracks by it. But it will stay with you as you go.

Myth: Ignoring grief makes it go away.

Suppose one day you broke your leg. Do you think it would heal better if you ignored it and tried to continue on with your life? Or would you seek help and get it treated, so you could heal? The pain of grief is mental and emotional rather than physical, but the principle is the same. It doesn't go away if you ignore it; it goes away when you acknowledge and treat it.

Have you ever tried to ignore serious physical pain without treating it? You may have been able to pretend it wasn't there for a little while, but then the pain gets so bad that you can't ignore it. At that point, you would have to do something. It's the same with emotional pain; you can probably ignore it for a little while, but the pain will be so intense that you can no longer act like it doesn't exist.

Trying to stifle pain often makes it worse in the end. Attempting to ignore your grief results in more severe pain than you would have otherwise. This circumstance is what drives many people into unhealthy behavior, like overeating or taking too many drugs and alcohol.

Instead, recognize what you're going through. The death of a loved one is a huge event, and all the emotions you're experiencing are completely natural in this state. Acknowledge the pain you're feeling and any other emotions such as anger when they arise. Feelings don't last forever, even though you may think they will when you're in the throes of an intense one. They will pass, as long as you accept them when they come.

Myth: Because you feel like you're going insane, you actually are insane.

It's critical to recognize that this loss is new to you. Even if you've experienced another death that left you feeling bereaved, you're working with a different person who filled a different need or role in your life. This is brand new territory where you haven't been before. The emotions, sense of emptiness and volatility of your particular emotions and thoughts are all new. You're not used to them, so it's normal that you feel like you're going crazy. This isn't the self that you're used to, and that's completely unsettling. You're likely having aches and pains that you didn't have before. You also probably have different eating and sleeping patterns. Your world is upside-down, and so is your sense of self.

Recall that these signals are all normal to the process. Grief manifests in your body and mind, affecting your nerves, stomach, and hormones. Of course you're behaving differently and not necessarily in ways you're proud of. When you start feeling like you might be insane because you don't recognize yourself, remember what you're going through. Look through the list of common symptoms and see what matches what you're exhibiting.

If everyone who goes through the death of a loved one feels this way, then either everyone is insane, or you're perfectly normal. Even though you don't feel normal in any way, shape, or form, these thoughts and feelings are what accompany the grief. You don't recognize them because you're not normally going through this process.

Also, if you can ask yourself if you're going insane—or you think you are insane—most likely, you're not. Mental illness tends to creep up on people as they dissociate from reality (Kam, 2014).[11] It's the people who are worried they're crazy who are actually sane. That being said, if you're concerned about it, you can always seek help and speak to a professional.

Myth: Women grieve more than men do.

Both men and women experience strong emotions, and both will feel bereaved when someone they love dies. This myth can be damaging for both genders. Men who believe they "should" be grieving less can be uncomfortable when the strong feelings hit them, leading them to deny or ignore their very real emotions. That, as we discussed, leads only to delaying the healing process. Women might feel pressured to display their emotions more intensely than they're comfortable with and feel that they're not really grieving "enough," even when they grieve in different ways. That can lead to unhealthy coping mechanisms and other issues that block their healing process.

Completely expressing the emotions is one way to move forward and often demonstrated by women. This is known as the intuitive pattern (Mendoza, 2018).[12] But other adaptive mechanisms include taking action and problem solving, which is often seen in men and called the instrumental pattern. The third form of grieving is a combination of intuitive and instrumental.

It's helpful to understand these patterns, especially when you're married or have a partner who is grieving the same loss. You may heal through taking action, whereas your partner could be expressing their feelings fully while on their path. Neither of you are wrong, and it's critical that you both understand what's happening.

The one who's intuitive often thinks the other is not grieving enough, and the one whose pattern is instrumental may think their partner is grieving too much. Once you recognize that you're simply experiencing different ways of healing, you can be less judgemental toward each other, which will help you both rebuild.

As with almost all aspects of grief, whichever pattern comes more naturally to you will be the right one. You could be a man who needs to express your emotions fully, or you may be a woman who prefers taking action and solving problems to help you heal. You could also find yourself with both needs. Whichever way it happens for you will be the right one for you, so don't let it stop you.

Myth: People grieve more when the deceased is young or they know in advance about the death, and grieve less when they know the person was suffering and death gave them peace.

This one is loaded. This myth, at first, may even seem quite rational. You might think—of course people don't grieve as much for someone who's been miserable because there's a sense of relief from believing the person has been released from their pain. Of course, people don't grieve as much for an older person who had a long and well-lived life compared to a younger person who could have done greater things. You may believe that when you know someone is dying, you grieve them during their illness, so you don't have as much to do after they're gone or you're farther along in the process.

Except that, as logical as these ideas may seem from the outside looking in, they are far from true when the experience actually comes.

Just as the journey of mourning is not linear, it is also most definitely not logical. Things that may seem to make sense when looking from the outside may actually be quite different from the inside.

When someone is dying, they and the people around them often start to mourn in the expectation of the death, which is known as anticipatory grief. End of life documents and plans get sorted out, and unfinished emotional business may also be addressed. Although in some ways, anticipatory grief does help prepare the people around them for the death, it doesn't necessarily lessen their grief. It's often still a shock when the actual death occurs, and the normal (as opposed to anticipatory) process begins.

That's similar to the experience of those mourning someone who was suffering before they died. Yes, there's a sense of relief that the deceased is no longer miserable and in pain, but that doesn't lessen the shock, nor does it necessarily lessen the pain that the bereaved feels. Relief is just one of the emotions that might be felt on the emotional rollercoaster of grief.

It doesn't mean that the journey of grieving will be curtailed or lessened in any way. Your loved one is still gone, and even if death ended their suffering, you are still in pain from losing them.

In many cases, because you love them so much, you hold out hope that they'll suddenly get better or recover and their pain will go away. Their death means the death of this hope as well, and that realization can also come as a shock that you weren't expecting.

Grief is also a process that you go through, whether the deceased is young or old. It's true that when a younger person dies that their potential goes with them, which can be difficult to deal with. However, your life might have been entwined with an older person's for decades, and losing someone who was part of your daily life is also very difficult. Either way, you're working with a void that the person has left within you.

Myth: You need to cry.

Tears are an outward sign of sorrow or pain, but not everyone experiences them. However, many people believe that you should! It's commonly associated with the intuitive pattern of mourning; although, those who take action may also find themselves tearing up at times too. It's also very cultural, since crying is considered shameful in some places, especially for men. Yet, some men will still feel better through their tears and shouldn't feel embarrassed by it.

We've talked about how you're often on a rollercoaster of emotions during your period of mourning. You might not be crying because you're not in a stage of feeling sad or overwhelmed. Some people cry when they're frustrated, sad, angry, overwhelmed, exhausted, or even happy. Others only cry with specific emotions, such as sadness. If that's you, then you won't be crying when you're on the rollercoaster with other feelings. If you're feeling numb, there may be no tears either.

Many people expect mourners to cry, which is reinforced by pop culture. You might feel pressure in doing so, since others are expecting it of you. However, if you don't have any tears, don't worry. Remember that others don't understand your grieving process or what you're going through, so their opinions on your personal journey are irrelevant. If you need to cry, then cry—that's the need you have in the moment. If you don't, then it's perfectly okay not to. As always, let your own patterns guide you.

Myth: The hardest year is the first one after the death.

Earlier in the book, I mentioned that the process can take about a year; that's when you may feel the most intense emotions. Your physical symptoms—such as sleep and eating changes—tend to be experienced during this first year.

However, that doesn't necessarily mean that the first year will be the hardest one for you. Because after the death of your loved one, you must then rebuild your life without their physical company. Sometimes, people find that aspect of recovery much more difficult than the year of strong emotions, so the second year or time they take to rebuild is the hardest.

Regardless of which one is harder, remember that it's a journey. It will take the time that it takes. Even if you find the rebuilding more difficult than the initial period of grief, you'll have some happy times and pleasant memories along with the hard parts. Just as you need to acknowledge and accept your sad and angry feelings, make room for the joyous ones as well. The ups and downs are part of the path—a feature, not a bug. Don't feel bad or guilty when you have good times during the journey because they're part of it too.

Myth: Grief ends.

This particular journey doesn't have a set endpoint or destination. You'll always encounter the sadness of your loss when you think about it, though over time, the pain will be less intense. You may feel that you've rebuilt your life and are handling everything very well, then suddenly a memory will arise and your grief returns for a brief time.

Anything can bring back the memory of your loved one. It could be a particular time of year—holidays can be difficult for a while after someone's death, including their birthday or the day that they died. You may see someone at a distance or even up close who looks like the one you lost. This has happened to me several times, in fact. You might be looking at a work of art and suddenly remember how they loved the color blue. It often happens when you least expect it.

However, all this is perfectly normal, and it will happen years later. With time, the pangs won't be as sharp, and you might feel more nostalgic than sad... or not. Just be prepared that when you've accepted it and begun to live your life in its new normal state that your grief probably hasn't ended completely.

When it does recur, the best way to deal with it will be the same as what you're learning now: to recognize what you're feeling and accept it as a natural component of the process.

Myth: The emotional wounds heal completely.

In one sense, mental pain is different from physical pain. Unless you have certain health conditions, your physical wounds will heal. If you break your leg, the cast you wear holds the broken bone in place, so the body can knit it back together. If you cut yourself, the skin will close back up.

Unfortunately, grief doesn't work that way. That particular emptiness left in your life from the death of your loved one doesn't knit itself back together. It will be more like a scar that stays with you in the future.

However, the pain that is a natural consequence of this void *does* diminish over time. As noted before, there will be times when the grief comes back, even years after the loss. It will come and go over your lifetime, but you will have the tools to handle it when it does.

Myth: The goal of the grief process is to find closure.

We're a very goal-oriented society. You go to school so you can get a good job to pay your bills. You date, so you can get married and have children. It's hard to conceive a process that doesn't end in a goal, but grief is one.

What does closure mean? One definition is "a bringing to an end; conclusion."[13] You just saw that grief doesn't have an end. There's no conclusion to the process. There comes a time when you will accept your new reality without the possibility of your loved one in your life.

Another definition is "a comforting or satisfying sense of

finality" (Deveney, 2020).[14] Although you accept the death, it doesn't mean you're satisfied or comforted by it. The concept of closure is an important one in many aspects of life, but it doesn't seem particularly applicable to grief.

However, you might hear this myth from well-meaning people. Closure is generally accepted as a good thing, so they believe finding closure in your grief must be also. It's probably not something you will ever attain, so don't fret about whether you've reached this specific milestone.

When you reach the point of acceptance and are ready to begin the new chapter of your life, that's about as close as you will get in terms of closure or goals. There's no end to the grief itself because it will occur again and probably when you least expect it. Your journey will continue.

Myth: You need a funeral to grieve properly.

Certainly—funerals can help mourners accept their loved one's death. They also provide a way for friends and family to gather and get back in touch when they haven't seen each other in years. Some people are comforted by ritual, and funerals are a well-known way to honor the deceased.

However, that doesn't mean that everyone needs one. Some people state in their wills that they don't want a funeral, and there are other reasons why there may not be one. It doesn't mean that the mourners can't grieve properly; it's simply one ritual that people observe, though it's not necessarily required in the grieving process the way, say, feeling your feelings is. If you can't make the funeral, that also doesn't mean that you're doomed to be stuck on your journey.

You can always create your own ritual that's meaningful to you if you miss the funeral or none is held. You can gather your friends and family together at any time to celebrate the life of your loved one, or you might find another way to mark their death.

Myth: You're stuck in your grief if you keep some of their possessions around, display their pictures, cry when you think about them, or still talk about them after some time.

Look, sometimes people do get "stuck" and are suffering from complicated grief because their mourning is so intense that they can't move on. However, that has less to do with external triggers and more with their internal process. You can absolutely accept your new reality without having your loved one present in your life and still keep some of the things that remind you of them around. Accepting their death doesn't mean you should erase them from your memory.

The fact that they're no longer with you doesn't mean they were never significant in your life or well-loved. Sometimes, memories can come out of the blue and startle you, and sometimes grief pangs even years later can bring you to tears. That's okay.

What's more natural than keeping mementoes of a cherished person? You may be keeping things that were meaningful in your relationship with them, or simply things that remind you of the good times you had. It's also very normal to talk about the people who are close to you, and if their memory comes up in a conversation, there's no reason to ignore it. If these possessions make you happy in your new normal, you should keep them.

It's also perfectly normal, especially after a recent death, to have a hard time keeping mementos around you. So, you might want to get rid of some of their possessions and maybe move the pictures out of sight. If later, you change your mind and seeing their pictures brings you joy, you can move them back. Whatever brings you comfort, do it.

Myth: After the death of a spouse, you're "stuck" if you don't start dating again.

The prevailing image of families in pop culture is that of the nuclear family, which is essentially marriage and children. There's unspoken pressure to be a part of a couple. That's changing, of course, but the idea is very much ingrained in our society. It used to be the case that, when one spouse died, people expected the survivor to remarry eventually, especially if there are children involved. "They need a father" or "They need a mother" were the key phrases for people with under-aged kids. Nowadays, that may not be so much the case in all cultures, but the idea that a young widower should "get back on the horse" is still pervasive.

It's absolutely the case that many do find new partners after the death of the first. Many enjoy being married or at least part of a couple, or they may just simply want to fall in love again.

Others don't, or they may just need some time single before they start dating again. Sometimes, the surviving spouse finds that they enjoy getting to know themselves again and establishing their sense of self before they find another partner.

It's absolutely okay if you want to spend some time as a single person in your new normal. It doesn't mean that you're stuck or that you haven't accepted the death of your spouse; it just means that your life as a single person is where you want to be at the moment. You might change your mind later, fall in love, or neither. All of these choices are perfectly acceptable for you. Maybe they're not what your friends, relatives, or favorite person on TV would have chosen, but that's not your concern. Live your life at your own pace. Don't let others decide for you.

Myth: After the death of a child, you'll feel better by having another one.

Believe it or not, there are people out there who think this is true and will tell you this in the mistaken belief that it will make you feel better or get over your grief faster. As you've discovered, though, the emptiness from your loss is specific to the person who died. You might go on to have more children, but none of them will take the place of the one who's gone. Just as you would with any other type of loss, you move forward, even though the grief never completely leaves you.

Because it takes at least nine months for another child to appear, you might feel better once the next child arrives, not because this myth is actually true, but because enough time has passed that you've moved forward in your journey. However, you might not feel any better, because you need more time to grieve, which is also okay. But your child needs love and attention, no matter how you're feeling.

Myth: When you have children who are also grieving, you must ignore your own bereavement and tend to theirs first.

It's true that children grieve and, just like adults, need support during the process. However, that doesn't mean that you have to pretend yours doesn't exist or it's to a lesser extent; therefore, you would focus only on your child's experience. For a number of reasons, including your mental health and that of your child, you need to attend to your personal process as well.

When you're on an airplane listening to the safety review, what does the flight attendant say you should do when the oxygen masks are released? To put yours on first, and only *then* help someone else with theirs. Because if you don't have enough oxygen flowing into your lungs, you will be unable to help anyone else. In other words, taking care of yourself first is the best way to make sure you can assist others.

If you're not dealing with your own grief, you can't help anyone else with theirs. As we discussed earlier, you could maybe ignore your emotions for a short time, but then they'll explode later. They could explode on your child, even if you don't mean them to.

How can you help your child manage their emotions when you can't manage your own? If you don't have coping skills, how can you teach them to your child? Can your child accept that it's okay for them to be sad about the death when they see you pretending you're not? Of course not. Children mimic what they see, and if they see you modeling avoidance of your emotions, they'll do the same with theirs.

You might also consider what message you're sending to the next generation when you ignore your own pain or pretend it isn't there. They might grow up thinking that adults should never show their emotions or there's something wrong with them for showing their own feelings because you avoid yours.

They know that you're not feeling well; you can't hide that from them. If you try, they might think you're lying to them, or it's their fault you're feeling bad, since you won't admit that it's due to the loss you've suffered. In other words, there are a lot of ways that avoidance of your own pain in front of your kids could go wrong.

If you think of yourself as the leader of your family, remember that the definition of leadership has changed, even in the corporate world. It used to be top-down, command-

and-control, but now, great leaders demonstrate that they have empathy and high emotional intelligence. Being authentic and able to show your vulnerability is considered a key leadership trait. So don't be afraid to show those emotions to your kids and let them know you're grieving, too.

Myth: Grief won't change other relationships.

Grief changes the people who go through it. The physical, mental, and emotional symptoms dissipate as you work through the process, yet the new emptiness that you're learning to accept does have an effect on you. If you change, then it makes sense that some of your relationships will change too.

In addition, as you've no doubt experienced yourself, some of the people you thought would always be in your corner haven't shown up for you while you were mourning. They might not know how to deal with someone who's bereaved and are too embarrassed to try right now. Other people avoid mourners because it makes them think about death and grief, and they can't deal with it. Some others may just be fair-weather friends. You may find you can't trust them again.

On the flip side, you may have become closer to people you didn't know very well before because they are by your side and there when you need them. In the course of the healing journey, people who go to grief support groups sometimes find lifelong friends there, which could be true for you too.

The people around you who haven't experienced the same loss as you have may expect that everything would go back to "normal" once you've started rebuilding your life. But that doesn't mean you will pick up right where you left off, or even want to, especially with those who bailed on you when you needed them.

Your new life means you get to choose the relationships that validate you, with the people who accept you as you are. If someone wants you to go back to you being your old self, you don't have to comply. You don't even have to be friends with them anymore if you don't want to. Find the people who support and cheer you on, and you can cheer them on and support them as well.

Myth: You'll get the most support from friends and family.

Most people like to think this is true, and in some cases, it might be. However, it also might not be, so it's critical that you understand that their lack of support is not about you personally. It hurts when someone you think is a friend just ghosts you as soon as they hear about the death. It also hurts when people close to you seem to be implying that you could have prevented the death (which is one of the lies you might have been telling yourself anyway). Another case could be that you're grieving "wrong," either too much or too little. And yes, it's possible for those people to be in your very own family.

Their reactions are not about you, even though they're aimed at you. They're very much about themselves. They may not know how to act around you or what to say, so they say nothing and avoid you. They may no longer feel comfortable around you because your life is suddenly so different from theirs and they feel awkward. Otherwise, they may not know how to deal with their own feelings about mortality, so they lash out at you instead. Their reasons could be a combination of these as well. Also, if they're also going through mourning, it might just be their own coping mechanisms acting out.

If you do get support from family and friends, that's great! Lean on them when you can. People love to help, so let them help you, and it will be good for you both. If you don't, you still need support, but you'll need to find it in other places. You could find it with a support group, acquaintances, professional counselors, or even colleagues at work. Grief is a hard road to travel, so look outside your friends and family for encouragement and assistance when you need to.

Myth: You'll find the best support through others who have suffered a similar loss.

It is possible that you'll find a grief support group specifically for your situation (such as the death of a child or a spouse) and feel right at home. It's also possible that you'll meet people in the same situation who are not supportive and don't help you. Again, don't let it discourage you. It doesn't mean there's anything wrong with you or your healing process; it has more to do with those others.

If one group doesn't work, but you think the format would help you, try another. Sometimes, personalities get in the way. You might remind someone of a relative that was mean to them, so they don't want anything to do with you. You could also remind them of a favorite relative whose death they're grieving. You never know what's going on with others, so just move on if your first few attempts don't work for you.

Myth: Faith leaders, doctors, and counselors all have grief training and can help you.

There's no course in helping people through grief that doctors and counselors are required to take as part of their professional curriculum. Similarly, no religions have grief counseling requirements for their leaders.

That doesn't mean there aren't courses in grieving that these helpers can take to understand the people they see better. Certainly, there are people who specialize in helping others cope with grief and have researched or taken classes in how to do so effectively. If you're searching for professional help, or looking to your faith to find someone to assist you through the process, explore those who have a background in grief counseling.

Otherwise, you could easily end up with a well-meaning person who tells you some of the myths that we've already discussed in this chapter. People who are qualified to help you are out there, but you can't assume that anyone in a position of leadership has this kind of training and knowledge.

Myth: What has helped everyone else will help you.

To some degree, certain healthy habits will help you as they help all who grieve, such as eating healthy, getting some movement in your day, and receiving support. However, you'll probably hear from others who've gone through the death of a loved one about other techniques that got them through it. Some of these tools may work for you, whereas some may not. Just because it worked for them doesn't mean it will work for you because the process is so individualized.

For example, Cheryl Strayed hiked the length of the Pacific Crest Trail in part to deal with the death of her mother, which she describes in her book *Wild*. But if you hate hiking, this method likely won't work for you. She did also mention directly that her hike was right for her, but maybe not something that everyone else should do.

Other people might recommend something like art or music therapy, which you might want to try. I myself recommended keeping the journal from earlier, but that might not work for everyone. People might suggest that you go to one support group or another, but in the end, you might decide that these groups just aren't really for you. They'll mention books you should read or movies you should watch.

All or any of these ideas might be constructive for you and help you with your path to healing. However, they may also not be. I myself have had good experiences with some of these, though not all of them. When you're feeling numb, it's often difficult to make a decision about what to do, but at other times, you can try things that sound attractive to see what works.

It doesn't matter whether the person making the recommendation is in the same situation as you with the same type of loss. You have different interests and values and need to do what's right for you. You might be surprised at how well a suggestion works out, or you might say, "No, this just isn't for me," and move on.

Myth: Some deaths are "better" or "worse" than others.

Welcome to the Grief Olympics, where you fight to see who has the best grief! The death of a child is usually agreed to be the worst loss that anyone can suffer, so the parent who's experiencing that kind of loss "wins" the competition for sorrow. Sounds ridiculous, doesn't it? Yet it's not that rare. A parent who's grieving a child—particularly a mother—may be given more latitude in their process than someone who's "only" lost a spouse or their own parent.

But a death is a death. Any loss leaves a void in the mourner's life, whether it's in the shape of a child, spouse, or whoever else. No matter what the relationship is with the deceased, you will go through the grieving process because that's what humans do. Your pain is your pain, and it's not comparable to anyone else's. It's neither better nor worse; it just is.

Everyone who's suffering from the emptiness of losing a loved one should be given plenty of latitude to grieve in their own way and on their own terms. Don't try to tell yourself that you should get over your loss quicker because it was "only" your spouse or parent who died and not your child, nor should you allow anyone else to tell you that. You have to acknowledge and accept your loss, regardless of who it was you lost, so you can heal and rebuild your life without your loved one. That process takes time and cannot be rushed.

Myth: Only a pill can help.

Yes, our culture is definitely focused on fast fixes. Many of us look to find a magic pill to solve our problems, whether it's weight gain, heart disease, grief, or any other kind of pain. You might even see ads for magic pills or potions when you're online or watching TV. They won't call themselves magic pills or potions, and they may claim to solve your problems. However, you'll notice, if you read the fine print, that even if these things are "backed by science" or a "natural remedy," there's actually no scientific justifications that prove any of them actually work.

To clarify, I'm not opposed to medication when it's prescribed by a medical professional. In this case, if your grief counselor happens to be a psychiatrist and they point you to a medical solution, that's fine. We're talking about those less-than-scientific solutions offered out there or—just as bad—self-medication.

People in pain want to get rid of it as quickly as possible, and we'll buy things that promise to do so, even if there's no evidence that it works. We want it to work, but you shouldn't have to waste your money on pills and potions sold by modern-day witch doctors and snake oil salespeople.

The human body—including the brain—has amazing powers to heal itself. I mentioned earlier that with support, broken bones knit themselves back together and wounds close. Smokers who quit discover that their lungs repair themselves from the damage. Liver can regenerate itself and neurons make repairs in the brain too. All this works best with a healthy body that's nourished and hydrated, but the body can still make repairs when it's not in optimal condition. Healing may be slower, but can still occur. Sometimes, cancer patients who are not expected to survive long without treatment end up having their cancer go into remission, which is another example of the body's amazing power of repair.

The reason you hear about the powers of all these pills, potions, and oils making people better is largely due to the *placebo effect*. It demonstrates the immense power of the human brain because people can actually improve their condition by believing that the remedy will work. That's why, in scientific trials for drugs, there's a control group that doesn't get the drug but believes they did because they're given a placebo, or fake drug. If the group that receives the real drug improves more than the group who got the placebo, the drug is more likely to be effective.

In other words, the belief that you'll get better is enough. There are proven methods for losing weight, improving heart health, and moving through the grief process, though none of them can happen overnight. Eating less and moving more is the basic prescription for losing weight. Getting more exercise and eating healthy is the best way to improve your heart health before it's too damaged. Taking the time to acknowledge and accept your loss is the way to move forward with bereavement. These are all time-tested methods.

I do want to address the times when a pill is necessary

again. If you're experiencing clinical depression, anxiety, or some other underlying mental health condition, medicine in combination with therapy can help. Grief can also cause some physiological conditions that may require medication, so don't ever doubt the importance of visiting a medical professional.

However, if grief is what you're struggling with, know that the pain does lighten over time. Instead of spending money on untested pills and over-the-counter drugs, try using your funds on things that you know bring you pleasure. For example, hobbies can be very healing during this time, so buy yourself some new art supplies, yarn, wood, or whatever you use in your craft.

Myth: The experience of grief will transform you into a better person.

Like many other myths, this one is sometimes true. Some people who go through the process learn so much about themselves and other people that they find it's ultimately positive. The experience can be transformational, even if it doesn't feel that way when going through it. Looking back on it, once you've built your new life, you may discover that you're more resilient, compassionate, or empathetic for example.

It's a popular idea because culture is pretty keen on self-improvement. If you sit in on any screenwriting or storytelling class, you'll hear from pretty much every modern teacher that the protagonist has to undergo a transformation. The hero starts their journey in one way and experiences a significant change by the end. That's known as the character arc, and it's pretty important. Grief fits into that narrative very well. In many character arcs, the hero starts off with everyone in their life, and then someone close to them dies.

They encounter situations as they grieve, and by the end of the story, they have improved something about themselves that makes them a better person.

However, that doesn't happen for everyone. Not everyone goes through a transformation or develops a new strength. That doesn't mean they did it wrong; it just means that the narrative doesn't fit that particular person. If you don't feel transformed or improved by your process, that's completely normal too. You're simply in a different story.

CHAPTER SUMMARY

There are a lot of myths out there regarding grief. Well-meaning people can tell you things that are wrong or won't serve you while you're undergoing the process.

- Some myths are true for some and not for others, so whatever feels right on your journey will be true for you.
- Other myths may not be true at all and should be ignored.
- Although many of these myths are born out of good intentions, that doesn't mean you should believe or agree with them.
- You don't have to stay in touch with those who try to push these beliefs on you, no matter how well-meaning they may be.

In the next chapter, you will learn about more ideas regarding grief that may not necessarily be true for you.

CHAPTER SIX: MORE POPULAR GRIEF MYTHS

Did any of the concepts discussed in the last chapter ring a bell with you? Have you heard or run across them before? It seems like a lot, but believe it or not, there are still even *more* folk legends and superstitions about grief. Hopefully, between these two chapters, we'll cover most of the ideas that can be most harmful to you in your bereavement. Having been forewarned, if you run across them in the future, you can write them off as stories that won't necessarily serve you on your journey.

Being blocked on your path to healing, whether it's from a false belief or other issue, makes it harder for you to move forward. It also makes it easier to fall into unhealthy coping mechanisms like I did. I'm hoping that laying these all out for you will keep you moving forward instead of preventing you from healing.

You may have lost an incredibly important person in your life, but you don't have to lose everything as a consequence of that. Grief doesn't have to be a journey that turns your entire life inside out and upside down. You do have the choice to learn how to heal healthily instead of going down the self-destructive path first. I've been there and do not recommend it! Ignore the myths that block you or trigger unconstructive behavior.

Myth: You need to be "strong."

Usually, what people mean by strength is a form of stoicism: not showing emotion, putting a brave face on it in front of other people, or otherwise acting like nothing major has happened to you. However, the death of someone significant in your life is a critical event. Something big has occurred, and as you've learned, pretending otherwise won't help you on your journey.

In the last chapter, we discussed why you shouldn't put on a brave front for your children by acting as if you're not grieving. Not only is it bad for you, but it's also detrimental to your child's health. Although your pretense probably isn't as damaging to other adults as it would be to your child, how does it serve anyone?

You may believe that your grief will only bring other people down, or you'll be a burden. But you don't actually have control over other people's feelings or reactions to you. That's up to them entirely.

Surely, you didn't go about your daily life before your loss and being only a ray of sunshine to everyone you meet along the way! Everyone has down days or times when we get frustrated or angry and express that to other people. You probably didn't consider that as burdening other people or bringing them down then. Maybe they were temporarily unhappy, but it didn't last forever, and neither will it last if you express your sadness or anger now.

To be fair, on the rollercoaster of emotions that comes with the process, you will sometimes actually feel strong. You'll have days when you feel pleasure, or your grief isn't as intense as it was on other days. To show that you're feeling strong when you are truly feeling that way is healthy.

But why do you feel the need to put on a brave face when you've suffered a serious loss, especially now that you know it's an obstacle on your path to healing? What is the purpose of being stoic? Other people know that you're going through this process, so why pretend you're not, or that it doesn't affect you when it clearly does?

The 21st century has brought us a new understanding of strength. Maybe it's time to be strong in a different way. Being able to express your feelings openly is a sign of emotional intelligence, not weakness. Showing up as your true self—even when you're feeling broken, sad, or angry—is an act of courage.

> ***"Vulnerability really means to be strong and secure enough within yourself that you are able to walk outside without your armor on. You are able to show up in life as just you. That is genuine strength and courage. Armor may look tough, but all it does is mask insecurity and fear."[15]***

— ALARIC HUTCHINSON

When you're authentic, you help others around you to be their true selves as well. They can connect with you much deeper, which will help you fend off the isolation that often accompanies your grief. Don't waste your energy in putting on a false face or pretending that you're whole and unfazed by your loss. Redirect all that time and energy into constructive activities that can help you heal.

Myth: The length or intensity of your grief correlates directly to how much you loved that person.

A popular idea in the business world that has infiltrated other aspects of culture is that everything is or should be measurable. This is typified by the business adage that "If you can measure it you can manage it." This concept is often true in the business world but definitely not when it comes to the complexities of human emotions and mental processes, which are what grief is all about.

Sometimes, people try to measure grief by the period it takes, amount of crying that accompanies the process, or number of stages that everyone goes through, all of which we've debunked in earlier chapters. Another form of measurement comes through this myth—that time or intensity is how you can calculate how much love there is.

Sounds pretty ridiculous put that way, doesn't it? Your love is boundless and cannot be confined to statistics and numerical calculations. The fact that the person you loved is no longer in your life is irrelevant because you'll never stop loving them; therefore, even before you start recalling what you now know about the process of mourning, you can see right through this idea.

Because grief is such an individual concept, some people will take longer than others. That has nothing to do with how much the deceased was loved, but rather with the time you need to take to move forward. You could love someone very much and still be ready to move forward with your life in a shorter time than another mourner might be.

The intensity of your grief will come and go throughout your life. Even before you're ready to rebuild your life, you'll have days when your sorrow takes a back seat to other emotions. You may be so busy that you don't have time to feel your grief for a while. That doesn't mean you never loved the one who died, are forgetting them, or loved them less; it just means you're experiencing a normal grieving process.

Myth: Staying busy will help you recover faster.

One of the reasons you might come across this concept is that being busy is important in our culture. People say they can't take time out for self-care or to be with friends and family because they're "too busy." It's almost a badge of honor, especially in the business world. Note that there is a big difference between being busy and being productive. The point is that, in general, staying *busy* is considered a good thing by many. Therefore, staying busy in grief must also be good, right?

Busy-ness and business serve as distractions from what's really going on inside your head. When you're busy, you don't have time to notice your emotions quite as much, though you can be sure they're still there; you're just ignoring them.

If you stay busy all day and avoid your feelings, they'll often come crashing in as soon as you get home or slow down your activities. It can make you feel worse than if you'd attended to them during the day and allowed yourself a little time to blow off the accumulated steam.

Having said all that, being distracted or busy sometimes isn't a bad thing! You might get caught up in a project at work or at home, or be absorbed by someone else's conversation or a book you're reading. You might even enjoy a movie or TV show. All of that is natural and perfectly okay when grieving. You don't have to watch sad movies or shows about people who are grieving, unless you want to. It's fine to think about something else besides your loss during your day.

Having activities that occupy your time is good for you while bereaved, especially healthy routines (which we'll cover soon enough as well). Just make sure you're not trying to distract yourself by not allowing yourself to acknowledge your emotions or stay so busy you have no time to pay attention to what's going on within you.

Myth: Time heals all wounds.

It's not the simple passage of time that will make your pain dissipate; it's the experience that you have along the way. When you allow yourself to acknowledge what you're going through and accept the feelings as they come, that's what helps you move forward—not how your loved one died last month and it's now a new month. Just because you've flipped over a calendar page doesn't indicate that you've made progress.

If that were true, you could ignore all the advice I'll be giving further on about healthy coping mechanisms and it wouldn't make a difference to your healing. You could engage in destructive behaviors like too much booze or too many drugs and it wouldn't make a difference. However, I can assure from personal experience that blocking yourself from healing does hinder your healing. Rebuilding takes much longer if you go down the wrong path.

Although grief takes the time it takes, how you work through the process will definitely affect your future. You can choose to go through it as sanely as possible. Remember that just because you feel crazy doesn't mean you're *actually* crazy during this time! You can also opt to place obstacles in your path that don't have to be there. If that's your choice, you'll find the process taking longer, and you won't start to feel better until you make a different decision about how to handle your emotions.

Myth: What didn't bother you last month or year won't bother you this month or year.

Because many of us tend to think of grief as a linear progression, it's pretty common to imagine that if you could get through a holiday or anniversary one year, that means you won't have any issues in the following years or months. You made it through the first major holiday, so you can check it off the list.

Did you think it would be that easy? For some people it is, but for many, the grief can come back with huge intensity later on. You've discovered that the process isn't linear, which means that if grief hits you hard on the second or third anniversary, you haven't somehow gone backwards in your journey.

This is a common experience for those who've lost a loved one. The first special day might have occurred while you were struggling to accept the loss. You might have been feeling numb or been in denial or anger for the first one. It's not until the next one that you truly experience the day without your loved one, without the feelings that protected you the first time.

The more you can accept your new reality, the more you can grow and transform as a person. You may handle more emotions at a later date and face things you couldn't face before. This is sometimes referred to as "peeling the onion;" at first, you can deal with the outer layers only, but as you develop your coping strategies, you can then peel back more of them. Sometimes, those other layers can be painful, but at that point, you'll know how to accept the pain and move through it.

Myth: If you had enough faith, you wouldn't be struggling so much.

Grief is difficult for those who have and those who don't have faith. Questioning your faith is a natural response to the loss you've suffered. You'll still need to go through the process of allowing yourself to feel your emotions as they come and cope with your bereavement.

If you study the history of your faith, you'll likely find others who suffered just as you do. You might find some fellow mourners in your faith group as well. Many people have doubts during this time, which doesn't mean that you're less than those who aren't doubting or haven't experienced the loss you have.

Myth: If you can't get over your grief, you'll never be happy again.

You've learned that you'll never truly "get over" this major loss in your life. The pain will diminish over time for the most part. You may have some flare-ups later when a memory suddenly reappears or on a significant or special date. Hopefully, it's clear that there's no "getting over," but simply "getting on" with the next chapter of your life. You may still feel that if you cannot accept the death or move through the process that you can't be happy.

During your grieving process, you'll find sometimes that your load has lightened. You'll feel pleasure in a familiar activity that you enjoyed before, such as a hobby, sport, or just having coffee with a close friend. You'll have those moments of joy and happiness. Unfortunately, they're often followed by a downhill trip to sadness or anger. Can you ever be happy for extended periods of time again?

Right now, it may not seem like it, but as you heal and learn to live with your loss, you will return to emotional equilibrium. It may be different from where you were before the death of your loved one; however, you'll be able to feel joy and pleasure without the pain chaser that you have now.

Myth: Living again is dishonoring the memory of your loved one.

Sometimes, people think that by being able to rebuild their lives, that their loved one wasn't really important to them. It may seem like healing from your grief means you're forgetting about the person who died, you should mourn them forever, being able to feel joy and happiness when your loved one is gone is disrespectful, or you didn't love them enough. In other words, something is wrong with you because you can move forward without them.

It's possible that the person who died would have wanted you to remain tearing your hair and rending your garments for the rest of your life now that they're gone. But it's more likely that they would actually want you to be happy, even though they're no longer with you in person. What they probably would want is for you not to forget them.

Moving forward into your new life doesn't mean that you'll forget them. The pain of their death will dissipate, but that also has nothing to do with you forgetting them. There are ways that you can memorialize them, some of which will be discussed in the next chapter. But even if you don't make a physical representation of your memories, they're still with you in the future.

The truth about life on this earth is that we die eventually, some of us sooner and some of us later. If none of us continued to live our lives after a loved one's death, most people on the planet would be miserable and lifeless.

Bowing to the inevitability of death and understanding that it's something every one of us will experience in one way or another is a healthy way to exist. Grief is how humans deal with mortality and heal from whatever loss we've experienced. It's a feature of life, not a "bug." Your loved one will always be with you—if only in memory—and you don't have to worry that you'll forget them as you move forward.

CHAPTER SUMMARY

There are many misconceptions about death and grief, and it's critical that you don't allow someone else's beliefs (or even your own!) to make you feel bad or guilty about your grieving process.

- Many myths stem from popular culture and well-meaning people who don't understand how grief works.
- You can choose to allow your process to work and rebuild your life—taking whatever time is necessary—by ignoring the beliefs that don't serve you.
- Rebuilding your life doesn't mean that you forget or turn your back on the memory of your loved one, but that you carry them with you as you move forward and live again.

In the next chapter, you will learn about healthy ways to handle grief.

CHAPTER SEVEN: COPING MECHANISM: WHAT CAN I DO?

At this point, you've learned a lot about the process of grief and healing from the death of your loved one. You understand that you're not going crazy but experiencing symptoms that are common for the bereaved. Hopefully, you've seen why some people may believe in misconceptions about grief. You are armed with the knowledge to tell apart what might serve you on your journey and what to ignore. In other words, you have a firm grasp of what's going on mentally, physically, and emotionally.

Having a handle on things is not the same as actually taking action to deal with grief though, so you're probably wondering what you can do about it. Many people fall prey to the easier and unhealthy coping pitfalls, such as overworking, overeating, or consuming drugs or alcohol. Those are all very familiar coping mechanisms, and you may have used one or more of them in the past. If those don't work, then what will?

In this chapter, we'll go over a number of ways to help you deal with your daily life while you're experiencing grief. You'll find some tools for managing your emotions without ignoring or pushing them away. In addition, there are techniques that will help you with the specific loss that will help you create memories that you can hang onto in the future.

Some of these methods are mandatory for healthy grieving, including self-care and learning to manage your emotions. You'll find different ways to handle your feelings, some of which might work better for you or seem more reasonable compared to others. Let your own self-knowledge guide you—coping is a skill like any other that you learn and train, but it is based on what works for you. Don't dismiss anything without at least giving it a try. You might find some tactics—foreign as they may seem to you—actually help a bit.

SELF-CARE

This often falls by the wayside because you're tired and can't be bothered to fix a nutritious meal or get to the gym. You may have lost your appetite and don't want to make food. You could have trouble getting to sleep because your grief keeps you awake, or you're so busy that you can't get to bed until two in the morning, throwing off your entire schedule. You might be too tired or feeling too isolated to call a friend. As you learned earlier, these are all common symptoms.

Taking care of yourself is *crucial*. You may or may not have other people to take care of while you're going through the process; yet, even if you live alone, you will still need to make sure you have a healthy routine.

No one—least of all yourself—is helped when you get sick as a result of not taking care of yourself. Grief affects the immune system, so if you're not treating yourself well, you will be more susceptible to whatever illness could be going around. By taking care of yourself, you can help shore up your immunity.

Your grieving process will certainly not proceed any faster if you end up with diabetes or a cardiovascular disease as a result of poor living habits either. Rather than sentencing yourself to a lifetime of medication (or worse), you can choose to take some preventative action during the course of your grief, so you can stay healthy.

Not only are there medical reasons for self-care, but there's also another important one: you'll feel better. When you're getting the sleep you need, moving your body and getting the blood flowing, eating nutritious food, and being supported by others, you won't feel quite as alone or bad as you would otherwise.

The following sections will detail the basics of self-care. If you can put these into a routine, you will feel so much the better. Because you are in uncharted territory with the loss of your loved one, it's often helpful to have a familiar routine that can give you a guide rope into the unknown. A little bit of safety in the form of good habits can ease your sense of having your world turned upside-down.

If you had a good routine previously, go back to it as soon as you can. You might need to bring back one habit at a time if you're having difficulty returning to it, and that's okay. Bring back the easiest one first and gently, establishing it before adding another one, and continue until all your good habits are back in place. Leave out the bad ones!

1. Move

There's a reason I didn't call this one "exercise." Many of us think of the gym, running marathons, or other strenuous activities that sound like they're way too much right now when we think about moving. Fortunately, that's not what we're talking about. Mind you, some people do find they feel better with vigorous exercise, and if that's you, go for it. Just make sure you don't overdo it and injure yourself.

If you had an exercise routine before, get back into it. If

it's been some time since you did it, go back slowly to prevent injury. For example, if you were running five miles a day, and it's been a few months since you did any running, you will be unable to run five miles a day again tomorrow. Build it up gradually.

If you didn't have an exercise program before, now is the time to go out for a walk. It's a great way to start moving your body. If you can manage ten minutes, then do ten minutes. You might also want to do some stretches once your body is warmed up if it feels good. The key here is to make sure you move—*really* move—each day. Even a little movement is better than none, especially when you're feeling fatigued. What I'm suggesting is that you avoid that tempting desire that could be lingering in your mind to just stay in bed. Start moving, slowly if necessary, and little by little at first.

At some point, you might want to do more. Go for it. The recommendations are at 150 to 300 minutes of moderate activity (breathing heavily but not winded) or 75 to 150 minutes of hard activity (breathing heavily and can't talk) a week, or some combination, spread throughout the week (HHS, 2019).[16] That's just half an hour a day of brisk walking, five days a week. The guidelines also recommend some muscle strengthening, which you can do with bodyweight movement.

Even if you have a physical condition that prevents you from walking, you can still get in some movement. I broke my foot and found plenty of workouts designed for a broken foot online. Whatever your issue might be, you can probably find something online to do.

By now, you might be wondering why movement is so important. As noted above, it does make you feel better. The human body evolved to move, not sit behind a desk all day. Some people like to go to the gym and "work out," but that's not necessary, as long as you get your butt off your seat and move it around.

Moving aids blood flow, and not just to the muscles but also to your brain, the latter of which needs highly oxygenated blood for nourishment. The better the condition your brain is in, the clearer you can think and make decisions, usually about proper self-care. You'll get more of the pleasure neurochemicals that make you feel happier. Blood flow is also key to keeping your heart healthy.

If you haven't had a movement routine before, now is a good time to create one. Your half-hour of brisk walking doesn't have to be done all at once if you don't have the energy or the interest in it. You can split it up during the day. Maybe, you can go for just a ten-minute walk before or after each meal, and you'll be set.

Walking doesn't require much equipment beyond a comfortable pair of athletic shoes, which most people have in their closet. You can put your shoes on and go. However, if there's a sport you like to play or enjoyed in the past, now's also a good time for that.

The good thing about sports is that many of them require you to play with other people, so you can get some human connection at the same time. Even solitary sports, like running or biking, have clubs you can join to give you that connection too.

Whatever you choose to do will be great, as long as you do it at least a little bit each day.

2. *Eat well*

Whether you eat nutritious food regularly, you know what it is: plenty of fresh fruits and vegetables, plus whole grains and lean proteins—all whole foods or as close to unprocessed as you can get. Sure, there are all kinds of diets out there and different ways to eat: vegan, keto, paleo, Mediterranean, and so on, but the basics are pretty clear.

As with many things, the occasional piece of cake or serving of French fries or frozen dinner won't do you much harm. It's when that kind of food composes most of your diet and you eat it regularly that you'll run into problems eventually. It's the same with alcohol; a glass of wine with dinner won't ruin you, but when you're up to a bottle of wine or more a day, you will probably have some issues.

What you might not know is why the stuff that's bad for you is bad—the processed foods, added sugar, and fried food. They all have adverse effects on your body, thus they'll affect your mind as well.

Take added sugar, for example. The sugar found in fruit isn't usually much of a problem for your body because it comes packed with the fiber and other nutrients found in fruit. It's the added sugar that you find in processed foods that's the problem.

People who have a lot of added sugar in their food have a higher risk of heart disease in addition to Type 2 diabetes. It causes inflammation and can raise your blood pressure. Because your liver has to deal with metabolizing it, too much sugar can also overload the liver (Harvard, 2019).[17]

Too much sugar can also cause a blood sugar rollercoaster ride, which isn't that great for your health. When your body realizes that sugar has entered, the pancreas makes insulin, which lowers the amount of sugar in your blood. Too much insulin release can result in blood that is too low in sugar, which can make you feel shaky or even faint. Avoiding sweetened foods when possible will help you manage your sugar intake.

Fried foods are linked to premature death in addition to heart disease and Type 2 diabetes (Ducharme, 2019).[18] Processed foods come in a wide variety, including many breakfast cereals, breads, meal helpers, and frozen dinners. To make them palatable and even addictive to buyers, they're often loaded with fat, salt, and sugar, which all hit the brain's dopamine system (Fox, 2018).[19]

Manufacturers often strip natural fiber from the food, particularly in grains. Many vitamins and minerals are lost during the process. They use *trans fats,* which are designed to make the food shelf-stable, though they come with their own health issues, including increasing irritability. Most processed foods contain a lot of salt, as mentioned earlier, and too much sodium has been linked to increased blood pressure—a precursor of heart disease.

You can see why avoiding these types of foods is so important. However, many people who are grieving have a problem with the nutritional food: much of this food must be prepared and cooked. In most cases, you are either too tired to do it or just don't want to.

It's much easier to grab a frozen dinner out of the freezer or stop at the drive thru, especially when you're fatigued. If your appetite's changed, you might not see the point in going through all that work.

Fortunately, we live in the 21st century, and there are ways to get around this problem. It's also key to think about things realistically. While grieving, you may be unable to avoid fast food or comfort eating completely. You just might not have the energy to go through with a meal plan you created when you are feeling fatigued. So, don't beat yourself up for the times when your meal isn't as nutritious as you want it to be. Remember that the more you can set yourself up for eating well, the better off you'll be.

- **If you're too tired to put much effort into your food...**

Order groceries online and get whole foods that are packaged conveniently. For example, you can buy pre-cut carrots, celery sticks, and whole chickens that are already roasted for you.

Some grocery stores offer their own freshly packaged food as well, like potato salad or soup. These might not be as good as having you make it at home, but because they don't have to be shelf-stable, they're probably not quite as full of additives and trans fats. Always check the nutrition info online to be sure.

- **If you don't really want to eat...**

Order groceries online, taking advantage of conveniently packaged food as above. You may also want to think about buying deli meats and cheeses. Then, you can make easy sandwiches, which, when made with whole-grain bread, can be nutritious and not take as much prep time. Foods that are easy to grab, go, and still be nutritious will be great for you right now.

Add in some foods that you know you like to encourage your eating. If there are foods you hate—even if they're nutritious—skip them. Get something else that's palatable and you don't mind eating.

- **If you're overeating...**

Yes, again will recommend ordering groceries online. That way, the tempting store setups aren't in your field of vision. Make sure you have nutritious things to snack on for when you're tempted to munch. Fruit, pickles, and celery, for example, are all good for this.

You might also want to think about meal prep kits. They typically do require some prep on your part, but you may find that preparing them will help you think about and savor your food rather than eating to numb your feelings.

3. Sleep well

Is sleep really that important? You probably know some people—and before your loss, you might even have been one of them—who brag about how little sleep they get. It's another "virtue" signal for an important person: too busy to sleep!

However, there are plenty of processes that are critical to emotional, mental, and physical health that can only occur while you're sleeping. Most adults need seven to eight hours of actual sleep—not just time spent lying in bed. Otherwise, these important functions aren't optimized.

Again, the occasional sleepless night—while not enjoyable—is unlikely to do much damage in the long run; however, it may certainly affect your performance the next day. It's the long-term sleep deprivation that's been linked to Type 2 diabetes, high blood pressure, heart and kidney diseases, and stroke, not to mention depression and suicidal ideation (NIH, 2020).[20]

During sleep, your brain can make repairs on a cellular level, which is important in keeping you healthy. It improves learning and memory while helping you control your emotions and behavior. Sleep assists your body in reacting to insulin and boosts your immune system.

Unfortunately, as you discovered in an earlier chapter, grief often affects your sleep patterns too. You might have difficulty getting to sleep, or wake too much during the night. There are a number of ways you can help yourself get a better night's sleep.

You'll probably need to incorporate more than one of the tools listed below, but they'll also stand you in good stead for your rebuilding stage when grief isn't affecting your sleep as much.

- **Journal**

Just as you learned earlier in the book, writing down your thoughts and feelings can be very helpful. If you find your mind is racing with thoughts when you try to go to sleep, give journaling a try. Once your mind has released everything to the page, you know you don't have to worry about trying to remember things.

- **Shut off the screens well before bed**

This includes your smartphone, and yes, I'm aware that you may be a bit unhappy with this recommendation. However, it could very well be the most beneficial, especially if you've tried some of the others and are still having difficulty sleeping.

Screens—including your computer, laptop, tablet, TV, and smartphone—emit blue light. Your body interprets this light as meaning that it's daytime. Therefore, it suppresses the release of melatonin, which would ordinarily signal that it's time for sleep. By removing the screens an hour before bedtime, you allow your body to recognize that it's time for bed and prepare for sleep.

Charge your electronics in another room away from your bedroom. If you need an alarm, buy one instead of using your phone. It's also not a healthy habit to wake up and check your email or social media immediately because there are better ways to prepare for the day, especially when you're grieving.

- **Watch your stimulant intake**

Nicotine is a stimulant, as is caffeine found in coffee, teas, and sodas. Make sure you stop using them well before bed. Caffeine can take up to eight hours to metabolize, which means if you want to go to bed at 10 pm, you might need to cut out the coffee by 2.

When you get better sleep, you won't need as much caffeine to stay awake and alert. Right now, you might feel like you're running on caffeine, which isn't great for your health either. More sleep and better or enough food can help you reduce the need for it.

- **Set a schedule for sleeping and waking**

And stick to it! If you go wildly off schedule on the weekends, it'll interrupt your weekday pattern. You learned earlier that having a routine can be helpful when grieving, and a sleep routine is key to that as well. It'll help your body know when to sleep if you keep it at the same time.

Make sure you're giving yourself enough time for the seven to eight hours that you need. If you must be up by 6 am to go to work, then don't go to bed later than 11 pm; closer to 10 is probably better.

- **An hour of quiet time before bed**

You could catch up on some reading, meditate, or use some other relaxation techniques during this period of the day. Let yourself wind down and see how much better your sleep can be.

- **Darken and quiet the room at bedtime**

Most people sleep best when it's quiet and dark. There are a variety of ways to accomplish this. If your room is loud, you could try earplugs or a sound machine that produces white noise or soothing sounds, like ocean waves or rainfall.

For a dark room, you can buy room-darkening blinds, shades, or both. You could also try a sleep mask, maybe one with a calming scent such as lavender.

- **Cool the room off**

Most people also sleep better in a cool room. Turn your air conditioning to a lower temperature at night. Ceiling fans can also help you cool off without straining your electric bill.

You might also need to cool off your bedding. I personally find microfiber sheets as an invitation to night sweats, so consider going with the more traditional cotton, percale, or linen instead if you have the same problem. Some pillows and mattresses are designed to be cooling as well.

- **Get sunlight when possible**

If you live in an area that's often rainy or overcast, this one might be more difficult for you. However, being in the light outside, especially in the morning, will help your circadian rhythm adjust to a schedule.

Being in nature has been shown to lift one's mood, so get out to the park if you live in a city.

4. Get support

Given that humans are social animals, it's important to make sure that you maintain some connection while you're grieving. In previous chapters, we discussed different ways to get support during this time, such as friends and family who will be non-judgmental regarding how you go about your process, others who are also grieving the same person, grief support groups, and professionals such as therapists and counselors trained in helping the bereaved.

You may have noticed that social media hasn't been mentioned, and there are a couple reasons for that. But the bottom line is that you won't get the support you need through social media (as opposed to online grief support groups).

For one thing, the purpose of social media for those who run the platforms is to get as many eyeballs in front of their advertisers as possible. The various platforms may have begun as ways to get connected socially, but the goal now is for them to monetize you.

The apps have been designed to be addictive and tap into the variable reward system, so you can get that dopamine release when you receive a notification (Anderson, 2018).[21] Frankly, this isn't good for anyone and especially not someone who's grieving.

Not only that, but studies have found that people who use social media can become susceptible to depression (Sukel, 2019).[22] Many on social media post carefully curated pictures of themselves and their families, which can make another person feel anxious or sad, even when they're not grieving.

Many others that you're following or "connected" with aren't true connections. There's no intimacy—at least with most of them—unless you're very picky about who you connect to. You won't get the support you need from people you don't really know, although they may be sending you condolences.

I'm not saying you can't join a social media support group, post about your feelings, or anything like that. You might find doing so can be very helpful. However, you can't rely on social media to provide the comfort that you'll need during the process, so make sure you're in touch with people outside of it too.

You may feel better knowing that others have been through the same process as you're undergoing right now and came out on the other side successfully. That's the basis of many 12-step recovery groups too; if someone who's very much like you can do it, so can you. The people who've been through it themselves can share what worked for them and what didn't—just as I'm doing with this book.

Whether you choose a group, some individual people, or a combination of both, having people around with whom you can share what you're going through is key. Sometimes, you'll want to talk about your grief, whereas sometimes you'll want to talk about anything else. Both of these are okay, and the people you choose should be able to handle either choice, as long as you let them know what you need.

Asking for help is unfortunately seen by many to be weak, as if you should be able to get through anything—even a terrible loss like this—all by yourself. But recall that we evolved to help each other, and that's how we survived as a species in the first place.

Just as being vulnerable is actually a demonstration of strength, so is asking for help when you need it. It shows you're not afraid to admit that you don't have all the answers, especially when it comes to grief.

Plus, people like to be asked for help, so you're actually helping the other person too. Just make sure the person you're asking is capable of giving you what you need.

MANAGING EMOTIONS

Just as getting the basics of food, sleep, movement and support will promote health, even when you're ready for your new normal, so will learning how to manage your emotions. Again, we're talking "manage," not "ignore" or "avoid."

- ***Journaling***

You've already learned that this strategy can be helpful. If you get specific about how you're feeling during this time, you can then understand what emotions you're actually experiencing. By writing them down once you notice them and without making any judgments, you can learn to accept your feelings over time without feeling overwhelmed or guilty about them.

If you're having trouble getting started, try these prompts and see what comes up for you.
- "Today my grief feels like..."
- "What I wish today is..."
- "I'm surprised that today I feel..."
- "Right now I really miss..."

- ***Reading***

Sometimes, you might feel the need to be alone, yet still receive support. Reading books on grief, in addition to this one, can help you understand what's going on within you better. They allow you to dive more deeply into the information available.

Many books will also help you feel less alone in the world; although sometimes it seems hard to believe, others have been here before you. What's uncharted territory to you at this moment has been discovered by the others who also had to undergo the process. They will leave signposts and guides to help you forge your path forward, even if it doesn't look exactly like anyone else's.

- ***Attitude of gratitude***

While mourning your loved one, it can be hard to

remember that you do have a life outside your grief and you'll return to it. It's also easy to spiral downward into sadness and depression and stay there for too long.

However, cultivating a gratitude practice can help you stay connected to the world, even when grieving. It will also help once you rebuild as well to put the right perspective in while life is throwing you curveballs.

There are several ways to incorporate gratitude into your daily routine while using it as a stopgap when you feel like you might be heading downward.

- **Alphabet**

Go through the alphabet from A to Z and find the things you're grateful for, beginning with each letter of the alphabet.

Like this: A for asters, which I'm grateful to see in the fall. B for bowls, because I'm grateful to my grandmother for allowing me to keep hers. C for car, and I'm grateful that mine runs well. And so forth.

- **Gratitude journal**

If you're already journaling, you can add this to your practice. If not, you can keep a journal just for the things you're grateful for. You can write them down as they occur or take time each day to think about what you're thankful for.

As with other journals, you can buy one that has a cover you like or use a pad and pencil or pen. Writing them down and keeping them together can help you when you're having a bad day and need to be reminded of things to be grateful for.

- **Three things**

Each morning, night, or both, think about three reasons

you can be thankful. If you're journaling, you can write them down. If you prefer, you can do five or ten items, but don't make it less than three. Some days, you may struggle to come up with them, and that's perfectly normal.

- ***Ritual or ceremony for your new life***

Rites and rituals are important to human cultures around the world. Creating a ceremony to honor your decision to rebuild can provide you with some momentum for your new normal while giving you a special way to honor your loved one.

If you have a faith practice, there may be some rituals or symbols that you can use in this ceremony. Many people like to play music, light candles or incense, and find an object that they can use as a touchstone for their new lives. For example, you might select a beautiful stone that can sit on your desk later.

You could have a get-together with close friends, release balloons, take a hike, or plant a tree or flower. There is even the option to write words that come to you in your grief on a piece of paper that you would burn or on a rock that you would release into a pond. Try anything that can symbolize your new life to you.

- **Breathing exercises**

Many people don't even think about their breathing, yet taking time to focus on it can be an excellent way to help you avoid reacting with your emotions or calm you down when you're feeling stressed and overwhelmed.

In addition, paying attention to your breath is a way to be mindful in the present. I've listed some more methods further on. Being in the present means you're not agonizing over the past or worrying about the future, so it can be particularly helpful while you're grieving.

Deep breathing is often not performed correctly! Many people tend to inflate their chests where their lungs are located and suck in their stomach. However, that's actually counterproductive to relaxing.

Breathing from your chest doesn't allow your lungs to absorb oxygen fully and release carbon dioxide. Not only that, but it stimulates your fight-or-flight response system, so you could end up more tense than before (Helbert, 2012).[23]

The breathing that will help you relax and be more mindful inflates your *belly* instead. If you feel your stomach rising and falling with your breath, and not so much your chest, you're in good shape. One way to help you make sure you're breathing from your stomach is to imagine you're about to inhale a very pleasant smell.

It's best to sit comfortably for these breathing practices, with your arms, hands, and shoulders relaxed. If you haven't been doing breathing exercises for some time (if ever), start off with the first suggestion, then choose from there once you're comfortable with it.

If you find yourself getting light-headed from too much oxygen, then stop the exercise and let your breathing return to normal.

1. Notice your breath

Although it's recommended that you sit in a relaxed position, this one can actually be done almost any time, even when standing up. It's a good way to give yourself a brief timeout when you start feeling overwhelmed by emotion. The first few times you try it, sit in a position that feels comfortable with your hands relaxed.

Some people like to close their eyes, whereas others

prefer to gaze casually (as in, not a stare) at a spot a few feet in front of them. Notice what's happening around you—the air against your skin and noises and scents nearby. Feel your weight on the floor or seat and how your seat feels underneath you. Allow yourself to become aware of all the sensations in your body. No judgment or criticism, just noticing.

Now you can turn your attention to your breath. In this exercise, you don't need to make any changes to it, other than merely observing it. Think about the air entering your nostrils on the inhale and moving down your nose and throat to your lungs. Feel your stomach and ribs expanding with the air. Next, feel the sensations as the air moves back up your body to your nose and exits your nostrils.

Continue breathing naturally, in and out, noticing for a few minutes. No need to change anything or stress; just breathe normally and feel your breaths.

2. Basic deep breathing

After you're seated comfortably, squeeze your shoulders up toward your ears and down a few times, then leave them relaxed and down. Notice your breathing and feel your stomach moving in and out with the breath. You can put your hands on your belly if that makes it easier.

When you're ready, breathe in, then exhale for a count of five, squeezing out as much air as you can. Hold for two counts, then inhale slowly to the count of five, feeling your stomach expand. Imagine you're about to breathe a beautiful scent if that helps you with your stomach breathing.

Repeat this process five to ten times. Many people find their mind tends to wander, and that's perfectly normal. Go back to your breath when you notice you've wandered and begin again.

3. Breath of threes

This is another breathing exercise that can be done anywhere is very simple to do. It's another good way to pause when you're feeling emotional or overwhelmed.

Inhale for a count of three, hold for three, exhale for three, and hold the exhale for three. Do this three times, making sure your belly is expanding during your inhale and your chest not as much.

4. Bottom-middle-top (three-part breath)

This exercise can also be done lying down. It's very relaxing, so you might want to try it before you go to sleep if you're having a hard time settling down at night.

Inhale, then squeeze out all the air like you did in the basic deep breathing practice. On your next inhale, imagine the inside of your torso is an empty space that you're filling with fresh, clean air.

First, feel the inhale in your lower belly, up to your lower lungs. Continue inhaling and filling up the bottom of your ribcage, then the top. As you continue breathing in, feel the air coming into your chest and up through your shoulders, allowing them to rise with the air filling them.

At the top, pause for a count of two. Then, exhale slowly, emptying your space from your shoulders to your collarbone to your ribcage, top and bottom, your lungs top and bottom, and out through your stomach. Do this several times. Your out-breath should eventually be about twice as long as your in-breath.

- ***Mindfulness practice***

Being in the present can sometimes be difficult, especially

when grieving. You may be ruminating about what happened in the past or finding yourself worrying about what your life in the future will be like without your loved one. Mindfulness will help you stay right where you are.

Making a practice of it over time can also help you identify thoughts that don't serve you, so you can reframe them more positively. Otherwise, you can simply choose to ignore the thought. You can put the thought on an imaginary cloud and let it float away, or on top of an imaginary leaf that you set into a river flowing away from you.

Note that this section is titled "practice"—not "mastery" or "expert." People often find their thoughts intruding when they're trying to be quiet in their minds—concerns about their kids, the state of the world, their underwear, or any other topic that might come to mind can appear while in this thought process.

It's pretty common, though that doesn't mean you're failing at mindfulness; it merely means your brain is doing what it's designed to do, which is make some thoughts. Just return to your practice once you notice the intrusive ones, which typically happen fairly frequently in the beginning.

There are a number of ways you can bring more mindfulness into your everyday life. Here are just a few to get you started.

- **Notice your breathing**

Yes, the same exercise described above will help you be more present.

- **Meditation**

There are many ways to meditate, and people often find that they prefer one or two to others. If one doesn't work for you, try another. Remember that it's fairly common for thoughts to intrude when you're trying to quiet your mind, so don't judge or punish yourself for that. Just come back to your meditation once you notice you've wandered off mentally.

If you choose meditation, try to set aside the same time each day for your practice. You could also choose soothing music and scents to help you.

1. Walking

You might want to do this one where no one can see you, because it does look and feel a bit weird. Warm up a little bit while walking for 10-15 steps each way, back and forth.

Now, you would get into the actual meditation. Basically, you would break down the mechanics of each step and perform each slowly, paying attention to your movements as you go.

There are four components of a step on each foot. First, the lifting. Second, move it a little bit forward. Third, put it down in the new place, heel first. Finally, your body weight shifts onto that foot as you prepare your other foot to repeat the process.

Your steps should be small and slow as you focus on them. Do this for about 10-15 steps.

2. Eating

Many of us tend to rush through meals, eating at our desk, computer, or in front of the TV. Choose a meal where you can sit down at the table and focus only on your food. Turn off the TV if necessary, so all your attention can be on what you're eating.

Before you lift a utensil, look at your food on the plate. Think about the work that went into making this meal. Not just the preparation in your home, but how the vegetables were grown and picked, and the animal's life if you eat meat. Think about the food's journey to get to your home.

Smell your food and observe the colors and shapes. When you put a small bite in your mouth, notice its texture and flavor before you begin to chew. Put your utensil down as you chew and only pick it up again once you've chewed it thoroughly and swallowed.

How does your meal make you feel? Were there any ingredients that you particularly liked or didn't like? Observe the entire meal in this way.

3. Mantra

Similar to breathing exercises, sit comfortably with your upper and lower body relaxed. Close your eyes or gaze ahead and repeat your mantra inwardly as you breathe in and out in a relaxed manner.

Your mantra can be something nonsensical, and should be very simple (like "om"), so there's no mental effort on your part to repeat it. When you start off, you can set a timer for a brief period of time—about five minutes—and work up to 20.

4. Guided

Some people find it much easier to listen to someone who can guide them through meditation. Here again, you'll find plenty of different meditation techniques and many people who do them. You can use apps on your phone, stream, or go online.

You may need to try several different guides before you find one with the style and voice that you like. If anything about their voice is annoying to you or rubs you the wrong way, move on to another.

○ **Yoga**

As with meditation, there are many different types of yoga. Even if you can't perform other exercises due to physical limitations, you might still be able to practice yoga. There are special modifications for seniors with arthritis, pregnant mothers, among many others.

It helps with mindfulness because you would typically pair your activity with your breaths, so you have to focus on what you're doing. The movements may flow into one another, or you might concentrate on one pose for several minutes, depending on the type you choose.

If the first one you look into doesn't seem right for you, check out other forms. You can find them online, streaming, or at a facility near you. In my experience, the teachers at a yoga center are more hands-on and will help you more with poses than if you take a yoga class at your gym.

MEMORIALIZING YOUR LOVED ONE

These exercises and practices, unlike the concepts we've talked about so far, are specifically about centering yourself. The following will help you center your loved one, which is to say, orient the memory in your heart and mind in a way that you know you won't forget them, but that will also help you rebuild.

You may not choose to do all these practices, and feel free to pick and choose. They're listed by phase of grief from early on in your process to afterward once you're moving forward. However, you might choose to do them in a different order if that makes sense to you, and that's also great. It's your individual path, and you get to choose what works for you.

1. *Early grief*

This is the period where you will be on the rollercoaster of emotions. You may find that some of these practices make you want to cry or scream. It's all a natural consequence of what you're going through, so don't worry about whether your grief is "appropriate" or "enough." It *is*.

These ideas can help you on your path to healing, even if they seem to intensify what you're feeling at the moment. Pick one or two and see how they go; it will allow you to express whatever emotions come up for you.

- **Make a character list**

It's easy to idealize someone who just died. You may find at first that you remember only their good qualities—how kind they were to animals and their habit of rubbing your shoulders just when you needed it for example. Or you remember only the bad ones: their impatience, sarcasm, hot temper, or whatever else you didn't like about them.

But neither of those is the whole story of your loved one. Humans are imperfect by nature, so you know they had both good and bad qualities. Embrace the whole person that they were.

No one else has to see this list (unless you want to share it), so be brutally honest in your list. Don't make them out to be better or worse than they actually were, but record the things that made them unique in real life.

List out 20 characteristics that you'll miss about them and 20 that you won't miss. Don't worry if you struggle with one set more than the other. It's pretty common, and the point is for you to bring back all your memories of them, not just the good or bad ones. Keep going until you have at least 20 on each side.

- **Write a letter from you to your loved one**

As we discussed with journaling earlier, it's important to write the letter by hand. Unless you plan on sharing your letter—and you definitely don't have to if you don't want to—no one else will see it. You don't have to worry about penmanship or whether words are spelled wrong, as long as you know what you're trying to say.

You can decide what you want to tell them, though many find it helpful to describe what they're doing and what their life is like without their loved one. Feel free to share your emotions with them, especially about their death and how it impacted you. The deeper within yourself you can go, the more connected you'll feel.

If you've never written a letter where you let it all hang out, now is the time. This tends to be a very emotional exercise, so don't be surprised by any intensity or unexpected feeling that shows up while you're writing. Let your loved one know what's happening as you're writing the letter.

- **Write a letter from your loved one to you**

You don't have to do this letter, even if you've done the previous one. If you choose to, it's best to do the letter from you to them first, then give it a little time before you would start writing again.

Allow the emotions that came up during the previous letter a little time to settle before you embark on this one. You might also experience some strong emotions when you start the letter from them to you, which is also normal.

Imagine that your loved one has read your previous note. What would be their reaction? It's okay if you think their initial reaction would not be positive. Write down what they would say. After their initial thoughts, would they have some comfort to give you? What would they want for you in your life as you move forward?

As you come up with and imagine the answers, make sure you write them down and don't just keep them in your head. Again, you don't have to worry about spelling or bad handwriting; just make sure you know what the gist of it is.

- **Photo array**

Coming into contact with the physical reminders of your loved one will help you deal with the loss instead of ignoring or trying to avoid it through distractions.

Some people might prefer to make a scrapbook, which I've done in the past myself. Others may want to make a collage, and you may have a completely different idea of how you would organize and group the pictures.

You can be as crafty and artistic as you want or don't want. You can buy a special scrapbook just for these memories, glue them onto a piece of posterboard, or make a digital album with fancy covers, for example. It's not important to make it beautiful, unless that's important to you. It's more critical that you face the reminders and accept whatever feelings arise during the process.

Gather all the pictures that you have of them, including the ones you have of the two of you, if any. Take the time to remember where they were and what they were doing as you create your pictorial. Laugh, cry, scream, or do none of the above as you work—whatever suits you in the moment will work fine.

- **Other arts and crafts ideas**

Some of these may also be suitable for children if you are working through your grief with kids as well. This will depend on your particular talent or hobby.

For example, if you enjoy painting, you can create a

portrait of your loved one with symbols or concepts that were important to both of you. Suppose you both had a love of horses in common. You might choose to paint them in a paddock with their favorite horses.

If you make jewelry, consider making a charm bracelet where all the charms relate to your relationship in some way. Musicians can think about writing or performing a piece that's special.

You can adapt any art or craft this way: woodworking, ironwork, needlecrafts, etc. It can provide you with a way to do something you enjoy while creating a lasting memory of your loved one.

2. *Later on, after acceptance*

You've learned that grief will always be with you, even after you begin rebuilding. There are ways you can honor both your own process and your loved one even after you've accepted your new life without them.

- **Legacy**

Think about how your loved one changed your life for the better. How did they influence, give to, or help you? Their legacy ultimately helped you become the person you are today.

How can you share the love they gave you? There are many ways you can give thanks while giving back, or pay it forward if you like to think of it that way. Give your time or money to their favorite charity. If they helped you in a specific way, how can you help others in a similar way that honors your own gifts?

- **Special dates acknowledgement**

Earlier in the book, we discussed how holidays and special dates like anniversaries and birthdays can be hard to get through, even after you've begun to live your life again.

Go through your calendar and see what days are significant and likely to bring up those strong emotions. Plan how you'll take care of yourself during those times and if you think there's a way for you to honor your loved one at the same time.

For example, you might know that their birthday is a very emotional day for you. Maybe you can choose to donate to their favorite cause in their name on that day and plan a trip to your favorite restaurant to ease your pain.

- **Helping another in their grief**

Even if you don't know someone who's going through a similar grief process personally, you can probably find someone to write a letter to. Offer them unconditional support without judgment or criticism. The more you can write with an open and honest heart, the more likely it will be for you to connect with them.

Although what helped you may or may not help them, you can still offer compassion and love. Avoid telling them what to do, but if you think sharing a story will be positive, you can do that in your letter.

You might choose to share some of the results of your work, and that's up to you. If you believe you can help someone else—and if it helps you build connections—the better. If you prefer to keep things private, that's also fine.

CHAPTER SUMMARY

There are many ways in which you can learn to cope with your grief as you travel through your process. Find the methods that work for you and can help you avoid the unhealthy mechanisms that will block you on your path to healing.

- Everyone—whether introverted or extroverted and no matter who they're grieving—needs to work on their healthy habits including getting enough sleep, eating nourishing food, moving their bodies, and finding support from other people.
- Learning to manage your emotions through activities like mindfulness practice, breathing exercises, and journaling will not only help you with your grief, but also when you're living your new normal.
- Other activities—such as writing a letter to your loved one and creating a photo collage—will help you create lasting memorials that honor the person you've lost.

In the next chapter, we will go over how to tie everything together with a system for acceptance.

CHAPTER EIGHT: THE SIX STEPS TO ACCEPTANCE

In this chapter, you'll learn about a system you can use for your journey that will help you deal with the grief and grow from the pain. By now, you understand the five stages of grief and the symptoms you may not have expected that are due to your loss. You know the misconceptions that often arise around the death of a loved one and how you can cope with your grief without self-destructing. Use those tools as you follow these six steps to the beginning of your new chapter in life.

1. Explore the pain and accept it as a constant companion.

In the previous chapters of this book, you discovered how important it is to feel your pain and allow yourself to grieve. Trying to numb, ignore, or avoid it will only slow you down on your journey to rebuilding.

Healing from your grief isn't a linear process. Although the five stages of grief are experienced by many mourners, not everyone will arrive at every stage, and most people will flow back and forth between the stages. Rather than thinking of your path as a step-by-step, forward movement, progress will actually occur in what feels like a series of loops (Begley, 2019).[24]

Therefore, there's no need to worry if you feel calm and accepting one minute and begin to cry the next. The key is to allow yourself to feel it all: the serenity, sorrow or frustration, and yes, pain.

Feel the emotions as they come, and they'll eventually start to diminish in intensity over time. Emotions are like a pot of boiling water: if you take the lid off to let the steam escape, it won't boil over, and the water will begin to cool. However, if you try to keep the lid on it, at some point, the steam pressure will blow that lid off.

Permitting yourself to feel is that escape valve for your grief, to let some of that steam out. Let those emotions out, so you don't explode. Having all these feelings is perfectly normal and a part of the healing process, so let them come and let them go as they will.

Your grief will always be with you. As you've learned, it can arise even years later after the loss and after you've gone through the journey to acceptance. With human beings, there's no "getting over" the death of someone we love, forgetting them, or letting go of them.

The bond you had with them doesn't go away just because they're no longer here. The pain you feel from losing them doesn't go away either, but over time, it will be less debilitating, and you will learn how to live with it.

Accept the things you cannot change. Once you stop fighting against the pain and grief and allow it to become a part of you, you'll find it easier to begin living again.

2. Learn to grow with the pain.

Now that you've accepted that grief will always be a part of your life moving forward, you can start to find the message and meaning in the loss, and how it can help you grow as a person.

Finding personal growth opportunities in the death of a loved one might seem selfish, but it's actually a way to bring meaning to the loss. Your loved one would probably be thrilled to find that their departure was cause for a positive change in you.

The message might be to take opportunities for love and connection wherever you find them, be more daring, be more resilient, or learn to be more adaptable or more accepting. You might discover a completely different meaning that you can use to be more self-aware and improve.

Grief is an ending, but it's also the start of a new beginning. Take the opportunity to make it a constructive beginning for your life.

3. Replace negative thoughts with positive ones.

Although it's natural to feel empty and alone and have negative thoughts in your mind when grieving, you don't have to stay stuck in them. As you move toward acceptance, it's helpful to be more pragmatic about the loss. The intense grief is temporary, and you will be able to live again.

The mindfulness practices discussed in the last chapter will help you notice these types of thoughts when they occur, so you can reframe them. The modifications should acknowledge what you're going through, not ignore the grief for you to pretend to be happy or force yourself to believe happy thoughts that are unrealistic.

For example, you might replace a thought about how terrible life is or that you'll never recover with something like, "This is a tough period in my life, and I'm learning how to move forward." Look at your grief journey as an experience to uncover knowledge from. "I feel sad today, though I still have things I can be grateful for in my life." "Now I know how to acknowledge and accept my feelings, even the ones I used to be ashamed of."

The bereaved can often reach a point where all they remember about their loved one are the negatives: what they disliked, their annoying quirks, the bad shared experiences, and the arguments. This is also perfectly normal and a good opportunity to reframe those thoughts. Yes, you hated it when they ignored you to watch TV, but you liked it when they gave you a massage at night.

The more you practice reframing your destructive thoughts blocking you from your path with positive ones, the easier it will be to catch them and recognize that the truth isn't so bleak.

Note that no one's asking you to change your personality or be someone you're not. You learned that your brain creates a lot of thoughts, but you don't have to attach any meaning to them. While you're grieving, many of the thoughts you're having aren't necessarily true. Instead of deciding to believe those thoughts, choose to modify them in a way that's both realistic and positive.

4. Fill the emptiness with the good, and release the bad.

That emptiness sometimes leads people to unhealthy behaviors like drinking and drugging, but you can take a healthier path. There are many positive actions you can take to feel good and no longer be driven by the loss.

Some of these are the healthy routines and coping mechanisms you discovered in the last chapter. But there are other methods that work too, such as finding a more fulfilling job or new relationships that can lift your heart and support you in your journey.

When you look at your life, you might notice that you have bad habits that don't serve you, bad relationships where the other people don't support you, or a job that doesn't fulfill you.

Sometimes, you'll want to let these things out by crying, screaming, or jumping up and down for example. *Let it out*. If tears help you get rid of the negativity, cry as hard as you like. If you can scream out your pain and inhale some peace, do that. Don't keep it in.

What better time than now to release those things and replace them with positive places and people that can help instead of hurt you? The more constructive ideas you can find to fill a part of the void that's been left, the easier it will be to accept your loss and move forward.

5. Talk about the process.

It's common for mourners to feel isolated from others and isolate themselves. Taking some time for self-reflection and honoring that want to be alone are perfectly normal and healthy, as long as you don't go too far and stop seeing or talking to people.

Speaking with others is a way to share your grief, and it doesn't mean you'll overload other people. Your expression of grief does not place a burden on anyone else, especially when they want to talk about it too.

Sometimes you'll want to talk about your loss or the loved one who died. But other times, you'll want to have a conversation about any topic except those two. Occasionally, you might just want to be in the presence of people who care about you—and whom you care about—without having to join in the discussion. All of these are normal and natural.

The death of a loved one would be a significant event in anyone's life. It's natural to talk about it, so allow yourself to do so. In addition to friends and family, you can look into grief support groups, therapists, and counselors. Treat it like the loss that it is.

Not to mention, learning to express your vulnerabilities is an important life skill. If you've had difficulty talking about your emotions in the past, you now have the chance to get better and build deeper connections with others as you do so.

6. Move forward.

Accepting the grief and loss is critical for living your life again. Expressing your emotions and learning to cope with them will help you rebuild and grow as a person. Your life may have been shattered, but you now have the tools to pick up the pieces and fit them together in a new way.

You'll bring your memories and grief for your loved one with you as you go forward with your new normal. They'll become a part of you, so you won't be leaving your loved one behind as you open up a new chapter in your life.

Allow it to be a healthy growth and the beginning of an even more meaningful life.

CHAPTER SUMMARY

The six steps to acceptance will help you synthesize what you've learned so far into a simple guide to acceptance.

- Only by truly acknowledging and accepting your grief and loss can you move forward.

- You can choose to make healthy decisions as you walk your path in grief.
- You can choose to make your new normal more meaningful and constructive, even as you bring your memories and grief with you.

FINAL WORDS

I hope by now you've begun to work through the process of your grief and identified the people who can support your journey.

There's a lot of information in this book because the death of a loved one is a huge and important topic to those who are suffering through the experience. You learned about the five stages of grief, which you may already have been familiar with because they're often mentioned in popular culture. However, you've also found out that not everyone goes through each stage, and that many people don't go through them in the order listed either.

Grief is a rollercoaster; it's not a step-by-step journey. Instead, you could move to one stage, then another, then back to the first. Your emotions are all over the place during this time, and they can be incredibly intense as well. Allowing yourself room to acknowledge and experience them fully is key to healing.

You also discovered that there are many other symptoms of grief in addition to the rollercoaster of emotions. Some people undergo a variety of physical symptoms, including stomach and head pain, dizziness, and nausea. Grief alters the brain's chemistry and causes sleep, appetite, hormonal, and mood changes. You may think you're going crazy because you feel so different, but you're not; it's just the bodily manifestations of the enormous loss you've suffered.

Some people also think they're going insane because they're faced with the paradox of wanting to be alone while desperately wanting company too. Whether you're an introvert or an extrovert, it's common to fluctuate between the two extremes. What will help you in your journey is allowing yourself to experience both sides and accept what's happening.

When grieving, you might come across two big lies that can sabotage you as you try to heal. One is something that you tell yourself: that there's something you could have done to prevent the death; however, there's no way to turn back time, even if it's true that you could have done something. More often than not, there's nothing you could have done, and this is just a way of trying to avoid the reality that your loved one is gone.

The other lie is one that you'll probably hear from other people. They'll tell you that the way to heal is just to "let go" of your grief, pain, and the loved one who died. However, detachment is also a roadblock. You will never let go of your grief fully, so it's only folly to try. Instead, by acknowledging and understanding your loss, you can move forward.

In addition to these two big lies, there are plenty of other myths and misconceptions that you might run across. By and large, they're said by people who mean well and want to help you heal, but that doesn't make them helpful. Western culture tends to avoid expressing feelings and talking about death, so many people believe that the various ways of avoiding or denying the loss will help. However, this is the opposite of what you need to do to heal. Lean into your feelings of loss and emptiness instead of away from them.

While working through your grief, you will need some healthy coping mechanisms to help you avoid falling into a trap of destructive behaviors. Everyone needs to build healthy habits of good sleep, good food, moving their bodies, and getting support. If you don't already have those building blocks in place, you discovered some tips for putting them into place.

In addition, there are activities such as mindfulness and journaling that can help you with managing your emotions. This is a skill that you'll need, even once you've moved forward with your life. You also found ways to help you memorialize your loved one and create lasting memories.

In the last chapter, you uncovered the system for putting all these ideas together and heal with the six steps to acceptance. Having a framework to follow will help you navigate the loss and grief.

If there's just one thing that you take from this book, I hope it's the knowledge that whatever you're going through and feeling at any given moment is the exact right path in your journey.

Although there are certainly commonalities to grief, everyone experiences it in their own way. How you respond to the loss could be very different from how you respond to a different one. What you're feeling right now is natural and normal for people who've lost a loved one, even if it feels terrifyingly different to you right now.

I hope this book helps you, I honestly do; if only a little, that'll still be a win. I know the pain of loss all too well, so my hope is and will always be to guide others through it and show them there is hope at the end of what might seem at first like a very dark and bleak journey. Please take care of yourself. I wish you well on your journey, and I hope this book has helped you along your way. Always remember: there *is* hope.

AUTHOR'S NOTE

Dear Reader,

I wrote this book from a place of love. It took a long time for me to do the research, but even longer to work up the courage to actually write it. To create all these pages, I had to open up an old wound and pour myself into the writing. It's an emotional wound, but that's okay. The pain and grief is a part of me and always will be.

We all grieve differently, so I won't claim I know what you're going through. I can only hope you found some comfort in my book. If that's the case—and if you don't mind—I ask that you please leave a review, so I know how it made you feel. I promise I'll read your words. I know opening up can be difficult, so I'll show you the respect you deserve by taking the time to read your review.

Thank you for reading. I wish you the best, now and always.

— JAMES WALKER

FIFTEEN POEMS TO EASE THE PAIN

Thank you for purchasing this book.

There is nothing we can say to take away the pain you might be feeling now, but we hope these fifteen classic poems will help ease the grief at least a bit.

Go to the link below to download your gift.

https://mailchi.mp/e99e1518d1ad/fifteen-poems-to-ease-the-pain

INCANDESCENT

REFERENCES

[1] https://www.psychologytoday.com/us/blog/ambigamy/201703/the-serenity-prayer-and-16-variations

[2] https://www.mayoclinic.org/diseases-conditions/complicated-grief/symptoms-causes/syc-20360374

[3] https://www.webmd.com/special-reports/grief-stages/20190711/how-grief-affects-your-body-and-mind

[4] https://introvertdear.com/news/introverts-alone-time-science-marti-olsen-laney/

[5] https://www.mayoclinic.org/healthy-lifestyle/stress-management/in-depth/support-groups/art-20044655

[6] https://www.newyorker.com/tech/annals-of-technology/why-we-need-answers

[7] https://www.newyorker.com/tech/annals-of-technology/why-we-need-answers

[8] https://www.neeuro.com/eight-reasons-handwriting-essential-brain-exercise/

[9] https://www.psychologytoday.com/us/blog/the-athletes-way/201602/3-specific-ways-helping-others-benefits-your-brain

[10] https://www.psychologytoday.com/us/blog/understanding-grief/201808/five-common-myths-about-grief

[11] https://www.webmd.com/mental-health/features/am-i-crazy#1

[12] https://www.psychologytoday.com/us/blog/understanding-grief/201808/five-common-myths-about-grief

[13] https://www.dictionary.com/browse/closure?s=t

[14] https://www.therecoveryvillage.com/mental-health/grief/related/grief-myths/

[15] https://www.xavierdagba.com/blog/18-quotes-that-will-convince-you-that-vulnerability-is-strength

[16] https://www.hhs.gov/fitness/be-active/physical-activity-guidelines-for-americans/index.html

[17] https://www.health.harvard.edu/heart-health/the-sweet-danger-of-sugar

[18] https://time.com/5509669/fried-foods-death-risk/

[19] https://www.active.com/nutrition/articles/10-Reasons-Why-Processed-Foods-Are-So-Bad-for-You

[20] https://www.nhlbi.nih.gov/health-topics/sleep-deprivation-and-deficiency

[21] https://www.bbc.com/news/technology-44640959

[22] https://www.dana.org/article/understanding-the-links-between-social-media-and-depression/

[23] https://www.goodtherapy.org/blog/breathing-lessons-0501124

[24] https://www.mskcc.org/news/coping-grief-7-things-remember-when-dealing-loss

Printed in Great Britain
by Amazon